Reconciliation

Toward Creative
Counseling and Education

Reconciliation

Toward Creative Counseling and Education

George Campbell Hage, Ed. D., Ph. D.

One Spirit Press

Portland, Oregon

ISBN: 978-1535363532

Library of Congress Cataloging-in-Publication Data
George Hage 2016.
   Reconciliation, Toward Creative Counseling and Education George Cambell Hage Includes bibliographical references and index.

   1. Psychology—Counseling   2. Sociology––Relationship with poverty and underserved. 3. Philosophy––Ontology; self dtermination. 5. Arts. 6 .Cultural Diversity

One Spirit Press
Portland, Oregon
onespiritpress@gmail.com

Dedication

I am remembering the graduate faculty with whom I studied at the University of North Carolina at Greensboro. Among this faculty, I am recalling the following, Doctors Fritz Mengert, Lois Edinger, Thomas Fitzgerald, David Purpel, Svi Shapiro, Dale Brubaker, and Dwight Clark. This faculty effectively modeled what education and academia in our schools should convey. I consider myself privileged to have studied with such caring and learned educators.

Abstract

This is a self-study proposing a philosophy, theory, and methodology for education and counseling. This depicts much of my education and philosophical background acquired through the years as a student of education and a practitioner of the same through teaching, counseling and ministry. The first seven chapters treat education in terms of a theory of Reconciliation applied to the human psyche and personality, and the last four chapters treat the resultant socio-cultural context of Reconciliation. Reconciliation depicts the joining of enemies through a truce. In this study it depicts the conjoining of oppositions in terms of segmentations in personality and culture. These oppositions are also depicted as antitheses that are synergized. The term synergized reflects the Greek term, synergia which denotes the living conjoining of differences and opposites into a state of purpose and harmony. At the same time, these differences and opposites maintain their identity while linking with one another through commonalities. In this study, this provides the means and purpose of education and counseling. Summarily, Reconciliation gives processual form, substance and purpose to the personality of the psyche. In turn, as the psyche interacts with others in the learning context, society and culture are also given processual form, substance and purpose. Interreflectively, the dynamics of psyche and culture creatively generate a portrait or composition of personality, culture and society.

Contents

Part One

Reconciliations
Recreating the Self and Psyche

"Knowledge is power. Information is liberating. Education is the premise of progress, in every society, in every family."

Kofi Annan

Chapter One
Assumptions and Knowledge Base

Reconciliation denotes the harmonization of differences and oppositions. It has also come to mean the finding of connections between varied ideas and belief systems. Obviously, this is the purpose of the United Nations and the Ecumenical movement; however, Reconciliation rises above politics and power. Rather it refers to acts of connecting the self with other and world apart from ulterior motives of power and control. To reconcile involves not merely sympathy but empathy, the ability to identify with the needs and strengths of the other. Essentially, it involves the ability to love the other as one would love the self.

In this self-study, Reconciliation implies a methodology of caring and reaching out to the other as well as caring for and reaching into the self. Reconciliation assumes the need for a positive and empowered identity that is derived from positive and effective synergism of self with other while including Being and Meta-Being. Herein Being and Meta-Being include the world, cosmos, and Being beyond Being with the assumption that the Being of insensibilities is existent and apprehended through the open heart of a human being, also called psyche and soul, yet when personalized is denoted self, persona and personality.

The Bible itself, especially, the writings of Apostle Paul focus upon Reconciliation as the work of Jesus Christ through his life, death, resurrection and ascension. Scripture teaches that with the fall of man in Adam, all of life and Being became afflicted with sin, disease and death. Ancient Mosaic Law defined the afflicted aspects of Being as contaminates or tebhel. The purpose of the Law was to preserve the uncontaminated from the contaminated, the pure from the impure. The contaminated depicts disease, decay, and death. In today's world, much of medical science is based on preserving the world from contaminates of disease but applying advanced knowledge and technology. Nevertheless, the essential principle remains the same.

As with the teaching of scripture, the essential work of healing involves Reconciliation, which includes preservation of the world from disease while healing it. This was the essential work of Christ, the apostles and the prophets and has also been the purpose of the world's major methodologies, philosophies and spiritualities. Thus Reconciliation must be all-inclusive. It must include the world, the cosmos, all sensibilities and insensibilities, nature and human. All of this indicates no exclusion.

However, as indicated through the fall of Adam, man's perceptions are tarnished and limited. Humankind tends to deal with difference as opposites. Small children in contrast with many adults demonstrate curiosity with difference, but many identities and cultures are centered on difference as animosity. The different one tends to be seen as odd, queer, and even to the point of Being sub-human or inhuman. Such a one is even looked upon as apart from and unequal with the animal and insect. This was certainly the case in ancient Israel with lepers, Gentiles and Samaritans among many. They were considered tebhel, to be feared, rejected and untouched. To draw near them was to enter their contamination.[1] Today we are encountering this same fear with Ebola as we did with AIDS in the recent past.

Nevertheless, Reconciliation leads us to rise beyond fears and to reach into self and beyond engendering a world of self and others

Mary Douglas, "The Abominations of Leviticus, "http://kodu.ut.ee/~-cect/teoreetilised%20seminarid_2011/teoreetiline%20seminar%20 15.03.2011/Douglas.pdf

in communion rather than at enmity. We must be willing to enter into the heart of tebhel with empathic love and caringness. We must engage with and invest ourselves in the needs and strengths of self and other, no matter how severe or limited, we must do this with the knowledge and gifts divinely bequeathed to us.

Likewise, I am applying Reconciliation through the fields of education and counseling. Also, from a strong theological and spiritual perspective, I envision the care of the whole over the part. Hence, I see counseling and teaching as caring for the self, the other and even the world, nature and Being. Although I am a man, and compared to the greatness of need in the world, I remain a very small part of it, but through education, I am given the vision of the whole and inclusive.

Over the years, along with other human beings of my awareness, I encountered much of the good and bad in the world. As a child, I was taught the value of taking the good with the bad and the bitter with the sweet. I was strongly advised that eating spinach, which most children of my day despised the taste of, was of greater importance than eating tastier foods. As a young minister, mentors urged me to deliver sermons that offer parishioners honey rather than vinegar.

From this, one may infer that the world of Being is dominated by the antitheses of good and evil, the primeval conflict. Nevertheless, one's self must endure the bad while sharing the good with the other. Through these metaphors, we are taught that the self must suffer evil while conveying good to the other. Often we are encouraged to love our neighbors and not ourselves.

Apparently we must meet the double challenge, which is, the tension of good and evil, and the love of the good for others over and against the self. Through the centuries, this latter assumption has come to mean the neglect of one's self for the other. From this, the ensuing problem has resulted in a nonself that is ever seeking self. Such a nonself depicts a vacuum sucking in whatever to grab on to. Such may be likened to self-gratification, but the seeking of such gratification never results in a positive self, namely a positive identity. Such an identity is denoted by "who I truly am."

Many in America experience this problem. Such people overly gravitate to the rich and the famous. They seek identity with rock stars, movie stars and the exceptionally wealthy. They remain not at home with themselves, and as such, a psyche has no self to be at home with. Thus they become overly ingratiated in a false sense of self, a false identity, one not truly belonging to them.

Resultantly, such a psyche cannot love the other as the self, for that Being has no true self to love. Rather such a love is false and deceptive. Such a one believing that he or she has love for the other actually is enmeshed with the other. This love is blind and deceptive as it tricks the "lover" into the belief that he or she is in love and being loved. In other words, this psyche is codependent due to loss in the other.

Hence, the ultimate therapeutic purpose of counseling and education results in the restoration of the self so that the psyche may truly love the other. Such a person is not enmeshed but truly loves because he or she has learned to really love the true self.

In Eastern Orthodox Christianity, we are taught the high value of dying to self. However, we cannot take up the cross daily and deny self with no self to deny. Thus it becomes incumbent that we first engender or create a self. Then and only then can we deny self by loving the other and the Supreme Being.

In counseling and teaching children, one guides them through Reconciliation. These clients enter the world innocent at birth, but through the years of development they lose their true sense of self. By adolescence, they are struggling for identity and certainty; at least, this is so in the United States. In contrast, small children intuitively know. They have a strong sense of self and world, yet without explaining it through adult logic. They fully experience the impulses to love and trust and the certainty of who they love and trust. They have no question about the self as they are bequeathed the self at conception and birth.

Thus counseling and education reinforce their natural impulses to trust and love with certainty, and even more so, to learn with curiosity and certainty. Children are endowed naturally and divinely with a clear, open heart and mind that work in synergy. As Adam and Eve are portrayed in the Garden of Eden, so children are endowed with the natural wisdom of innocence. They are able to learn with greater ease through questioning, mimesis and adaptation.

Yet, by the time they reach the upper grades of elementary school, through middle school and high school, the fire of their natural instincts is quenched. Their power to learn is decreased as indicated in the loss of their language acquisition factor. They are stringently forced to reason and learn as adults. They must memorize and pass tests. They are forced into adult identity at the expense of their God-given attributes. They are disabled from growing into the true wisdom and righteousness that belongs to them. Instead they are forced to embrace a false self, a personality and way of being that is unnatural to the human being.

Instead of truly loving, human beings enter into a culture of loss. As the ancient Jews who were reared in the rigors of the Law of Moses, children are still driven into such rigors. These rigors define and impose evil on their hearts and minds. They instill much that is wrong and stifling. Innocence is quenched for a false sense of righteousness and goodness. Curiosity is quenched for the imposition of what adult culture says is true and false, right and wrong, and through all of this stifling, the power of creativity is hindered and even quenched. Creativity coincides with the power of the language acquisition factor, curiosity, and open-ended pliability and adaptability.

In this light, guiding children through Reconciliation assumes they are already reconciled to self, other, and Being. Effective education and counseling preserves this state of Being with and in them while permitting them to mature into adolescence and adulthood. Hence, education and counseling must free themselves from the impact of traditional adult culture and society. This is as if we must maintain an ever-expanding cacoon of childhood through adulthood at which point the whole and transfigured human may emerge. Like the fully-grown butterfly, the human persona and self is fully empowered to wisdom, love and wholeness of self, other and Being. The full creative power of the self is unleashed bringing Reconciliation and restoration to a fallen world trapped in legalism—a legalism that empowers disease, evil and death, by defining and glorifying them at the expense of the good, the virtuous and the whole.

At this juncture, a thesis of need is proposed. This is a monastic type of counseling and education, which frees children from the current adult world and therefrom engenders a new world and new creation. For example, Jesus Christ came to earth offering Israel and the world a way of newness through Reconciliation, but the world of that day would not receive it. Regardless of their decision, it is not too late. Today, we may agree to change and implement such an education for children.

Nevertheless, we counselors and educators find ourselves working with what we have rather than *what we **ought** to have*. We are working in an adult culture with children who have been drastically impacted for the worse, so we must work with what we have. We must mold children as they are in a world as it is.

We have considered children *as they are* as well as *what they **ought** to be*. At this point, we are considering the worldview that children are reared in. Awareness of this reality is necessary in order to bring effective and positive change. Earlier we suggested the problem as Being summed up in the primeval conflict. This is the tension of good and evil in terms of antitheses permeating much of world cultures, especially American culture.

An underlying assumption of this study is that latent in the knowledge of problems is their solution. This is especially true of mental health. The clinician must grasp the problem of the client firmly in order to derive an effective treatment plan. The modus operandi of the treatment plan presents a client-centered paradigm of creative engagement with client strengths and needs. Through this process, he or she is empowered into a solution that reconciles the client with a positive sense of self and world.

Likewise we must grasp the overarching problem of Being in order to engender a paradigmatic methodology of change through education and counseling. Relatively, another major assumption of this study posits that adherence to the antithetical opposites of good and evil empower enmity of self with psyche, self with other, and self with Being and world. As noted, this self, in reality, is much of the time a nonself. This results in the capitulation of psyche to enmity, thereby afflicting it with traits and symptoms of disease and death.

This dynamic of the eternal and primeval conflict continues as the implicit dynamic behind our hopes, dreams and fears of loss. Here this antithesis is submitted as the vital heart of psyche and Being with the resultant challenge of reconciling the opposites reflected in this conflict. This is the dynamic of creative healing with counseling and education being applied to this end.

Concomitantly, the dynamics of conflict intertwine with the trials of life, which afflict us daily in both small and great ways. This is very true in our lives as well as the lives of our clients and students, yet as counselors and educators, we are available to care. In this light, the concept *educare* is proposed because it aptly defines the healing dimension of education as leading one through learning to healing. *Educare* denotes the present active infinitive of the Latin verb educo meaning to bring up, train or teach.[2]

In this study, emphasis is Being placed on "to bring up" as education not only involves the act of teaching but also that of nurturing.

2 *Educare*, http://en.wiktionary.org/wiki/educare (accessed December 23, 2014)

The whole person is taken into consideration as the whole organism is learning through developing. This total process is referred to as maturation. Through education, counseling also involves the facilitation of learning in the human being, which encompasses the spiritual, mental, physical and psychological dimensions.

With learning involving the psyche's acquisition of knowledge relative to cognitive and affective domains, the apprehension and comprehension of knowledge is referred to as understanding. At the same time, understanding depicts the reconciling of opposite poles without losing the character of the opposites. Understanding, in reality, manifests the balance of opposites as differences and with distinctions and connections.

Such Reconciliation denotes the ambivalence of the paradox. The meaningful paradox suggests the interconnections of opposites in terms of difference. Herein Reconciliation depicts the paradox as the source of all learning, meaning and creativity and healing.

One's apprehension of the paradox indicates the understanding of Being and world as truly not absolute or exact due to the fallibility of the human psyche. Herewith fallibility may likely be perpetuated by the psyche's tendency to be at rest while yet all things including the psyche continue in a state of conflicting motion.

Yet, if conflict were absent, Being would be vacuum, i.e., emptiness or nothingness. Perhaps upon the first day of creation God spoke motion into existence, thereby, eliciting Being. Relatively, from nothing all things proceed in terms of the negative/positive. Although the negative/positive is antithetical, these oppositions also suggest the essence of difference, thereby posing their terminus of synergy, hence, the paradox. All that is Being is life, and life is substantially conflict; hence, all humanity learns and matures through conflict. The antitheses or conflicts of life, resulting from the cosmic antithesis, are synonymous with reality. Underscoring this dynamic is Newton's Third Law of Motion: "Whenever one body exerts a force on a second body, the second body exerts an equal and opposite force on the first." [3]

Figure 1: The Cosmic Paradox

Epiphenomena

Eternity/Infinity---------------Ontic---------------Eternity/Infinity

Time and Matter

Eternity/Infinity   Life----------------Death   Eternity/Infinity

Time and Matter

Eternity/Infinity--------------Entic --------------Eternity/Infinity

Phenomena

The paradox demonstrates the inexactness and lack of finality in human knowledge and yet results from the reconciling of opposites. The process of reconciling is a creative act engendering learning, development and healing throughout the life of the psyche. Cross posits learning as a lifelong process.[4] In fact, learning reflects individuating in that every psyche's conflict with and in Being is unique. Consequently, the persona as personality must

---

3 bPaul G. Hewitt, *Conceptual Physics: A New Introduction to Your Environment.* Fourth Edition. Boston, Massachusetts: Little Brown and Company, 1981, p 36.
4 Patricia K. Cross, *Adults as Learners*: San Francisco: Jossey-Bass Publishers, 1981 cf. Ronald Gross, The *Lifelong Learner*. New York: The World Publishing Company, 1960.

choose ways and means that facilitate learning.

Fundamental to the humanity of the psyche moves the function of volition, and with interest, is the motivating factor in learning, development and healing. Sound education and counseling facilitate volition in the client and student. Volition in the personality and psyche is an innate right and characteristic of humanity. Volition with interest provides the impetus and directive movement of creativity through the learning, developmental and healing process.

Allowing ways of choice in learning empowers the psyche and personality with the will and choice of becoming. Such freedom of choice in learning enhances and facilitates psyche and personality into a balanced universal view of life and Being, therefore, empowering positive coping and management of self and world.

The process of learning is in reality *synergia*, which in English is read as synergy, synergization, and synergizing.[5] The closest English understanding is demonstrated by the cooperation of opposites, such as the paradox.

Relatively, all that is of phenomena and epiphenomena become in reality opposing poles or contrasts. Through Reconciliation, synergy creates the cooperation of opposites as differences. At the same time, the conflict of opposites is equal to energy and motion, which, in turn, is equal to life. Yet, in the synergetic dynamic, the tension of conflict continues but as indicated in the *both-and* paradox rather than the *either-or* paradox.

Nicholas of Cusa (14th century) denotes the paradox as *coincidentia oppositorum*. This is the meeting of opposites as the coincidence of contrasting ideas. Paradox manifests through *both-and* and *either-or* devices. The former is described as *elemental* and the

5 *Synergy*, http://en.wikipedia.org/wiki/Synergy (accessed December 24, 2014) cf. William F. Arndt and F. Wilbur Gingrich, *A Greek-English Lexicon of the New Testament and Other Early Christian Literature.* Chicago: The University of Chicago Press, 1957,

latter coincidental. He considers *either-or,* the meeting of opposites as an *exception* to the rule or norm in that oppositions are stressed over and against their relationship. He considers both/and and neither-nor as the rational synthesis of minimally opposing objects. Hence both-and and neither-nor devices remain paradoxical. Neither-nor reflects not either one not-or the other **one** [6] suggesting a negative approach to the positive both-and. All elements move gradually to the both-and paradox.[7]

The behavior of each human being involves interacting conflicts of personality and psyche with the conflicts of Being. The totality of human being and behavior is cumulative in the psyche and personality, thereby, reflective of maturation and individuating through learning. Therefrom the teleology of education and counseling derives meaning through conflict resulting in the synergy of opposites, in turn, giving meaning to the paradox.

Images reflect the positives of negatives impressed upon the personality during conflicts of the psyche and personality with the process of reconciling and synergizing opposites. Images are manifested in terms of the following processes: percepts become concepts; concepts become beliefs and assumptions; beliefs and assumptions become philosophies, perspectives and/or universal meaning systems.

In summation, the Hegelian dialectic of conflict with Reconciliation (thesis, antithesis, and synthesis), summarily, explains the learning process and development of personality and psyche. Each experience of the psyche and personality is a crisis of conflict whether minimal or maximal as defined by the psychodynamics of culture and psyche resulting in learning, development and phases of maturity in personality and psyche. Thus the self and persona mediate conflict through the reconciliatory process of the Hege-

---

6 Neither, http://www.thefreedictionary.com/neither (accessed December 14, 2014)
7 Howard A. Slaate, *The Pertinence of the Paradox.* New York: Humanities Press, 1968, p. 5

lian dialectic.

In coping, the personality and psyche choose to engage in conflict striving for the synergism of opposites, thereby, engendering
the paradox. In choosing not to cope, the personality and psyche
remain in oppositional and irreconcilable behavior either through
direct aggression, indirect aggression or total avoidance. Such oppositional and irreconcilable behavior over time most likely engenders imbalance in the personality and psyche while disempow-
ering the positive ability to cope with and manage self and world.

The choice to learn not only is aroused through conflicts, external and internal, with the self, but curiosity provokes within self
the challenge to learn. This challenge, often as an inadvertent opposite, naturally drives the personality and psyche to synergize its
opposite with the self in order to engender the paradox of meaning. As Brunner suggests: choosing to learn is aroused by curiosity,
and curiosity, in turn, results from boredom.[8]

In early childhood, differences arouse curiosity in the psyche.
The primordial inclination of the psyche sees differences as opposing poles to the self. Curiosity does not assume differences as
oppositional. Curiosity, an innate construct of the psyche from
childhood, is often minimized and even quenched through adolescence. Hence, to reject curiosity is the rejection of all conflict.
Ultimately such rejection is opposition in that rejection engenders
irreconcilable behavior. Thus the potential for meaning is lost engendering meaninglessness and nonsense. Paradox, therefore, becomes nonexistent.

Struggling to accept or reject curiosity and conflict is the antithesis of choice between accepting curiosity and conflict and re-
jecting curiosity and conflict. Rejection is as avoidance, therefore,
resulting in meaninglessness and nonsense. Accepting is engaging
synergistically, therefore, resulting in meaning and sense engendering the paradox.

---

8 Jerome S. Brunner, *Toward A Theory of Instruction*. Cambridge, Massachusetts: The Belknap Press of Harvard University Press, 1966, p. 112f.

Figure 2: Sense and Nonsense

Thesis→Antithesis→Synthesis

$$X_1 \rightarrow \leftarrow X_2 \rightarrow X_{1+2}$$

Self (personality and psyche)$_1$ →←Opposite$_2$→Learning$_{1+2}$

Self (personality and psyche)$_1$→←Opposite$_2$→Meaninglessness $_{1+2}$

Self→←Boredom→Curiosity

Self$_1$→←Curiosity$_2$ →Learning (Meaning) $_{1+2}$

Boredom depicts non-Being or nonexistence, that is, vacuum. From this void flows Being and knowledge, as from 0 begins all positive/negative quantities (objects) beginning with 1,-1,

Image (ikonos) depicts representations of things comprising Being and Meta Being... Conversely, Genesis 1 conveys the human being as the image of God (the Unknown Quantity [Being]). Hence, the essence of Being is unsensed, therefore, unknown, imaging the quantity 0, the essential "gap" in life and Being.

Brubaker defines learning as making sense out of "experiences or encounters with self, other, and the environment." [9] The assumptions of making sense depict the psyche's encountering opposites of self and synthesizing them into a meaningful whole, a gestalt. This whole depicts the either-or paradox being synthesized into neither/nor or both/and paradoxes.

Curriculum denotes the experience of self in a setting.[10] In concurrence with Brubaker, curriculum icons life in world and culture and simulates life in the context of setting. Curriculum sets the context for learning of the psyche within a school environment.

9 Dale L. Brubaker, *Curriculum Planning: The Dynamics of Theory and Practice*. Dallas Texas: Scott, Foresman and Company, 1982, p. 3.
10 Op. cit., p. 2.

Therefore, counseling of the psyche interreflects with his or her school curriculum.

Mind reflects the power of the persona or self to sense and conceptualize life and world through synthesis or synergy. Heart reflects the emotional life of mind. The essence and power of learning is enhanced and facilitated through the synergy of heart and mind. The psyche and person feels through thinking and thinks through feeling. Such a self is likened to the mystic and the artist.

Brubaker and Berger agree from the standpoints of education and sociology, that the autobiography is the vital source of developing the wholeness of meaning in life. Universal meaning systems are derived from biography and autobiography.[11] Both speak of universal meaning systems as worldview, namely, Weltanschauung. This concept denotes the dynamics of the universal meaning system reflected in biography and autobiography.[12]

The shape of human history interreflects with biography and autobiography. History, as indicated by the Hegelian dialectic, presents a paradigm for the psyche's human history and also his or her human development through learning. Development and maturation of the psyche interreflects with human history.

---

11 Brubaker, Op cit. cf. Peter L. Berger, *Invitation to Sociology: A Humanistic Perspective*. New York: Doubleday and Company, Inc., 1963.
12 Berger, Op. cit., p. 61 cf. Brubaker, Op. cit.

Notes

The highest levels of performance come to people who are centered, intuitive, creative, and reflective - people who know to see a problem as an opportunity.

Deepak Chopra

Chapter Two
The Proposition

Life is energy at work. Energy results from the dynamics of the ontological conflict, i.e., the antitheses among all epiphenomena and phenomena. The tension of struggle between a thesis and antithesis exerts force and movement (energia), the characteristics of life. Without antitheses life would be nonexistent, that is, Being would be non-Being or vacuum.

Such conflict is demonstrated in the either-or or both-and paradoxes. These are exemplified by the opposites of love and/or hate, good and/or evil, past and/or future, time and/or eternity, man and/or woman, wise and/or foolish, knowledge and/or ignorance, the dialectic of question and/or answer, etc. Consequently, a man and/or woman (the psyche) cannot truly avoid conflict. Rather he and/or she is/are in and of conflict. Although a man and/or woman is/are endowed with volition, if he and/or she resist(s) conflict he and/or she is/are still in conflict with the conflict. On the other hand, if a man and/or woman accept(s) conflict, he and/or she enter(s) into it.

Throughout the biography of the psyche, choice remains an integral part of the persona. On the other hand, to have no choice is to have no independent being or existence. Consequently, being without choice is to be subject to the whole of cosmic energy, which for the psyche would be the same as nonexistence. Choice may not be rejected. It remains an integral part of the persona.

Learning begins the "moment" the persona encounters cosmic energy (life) in the womb. The persona always chooses even when the psyche in consciousness is unaware of the choice. The behavior of the psyche commences and is shaped around choice. As the persona attains the knowledge of choice, the psyche learns regardless of the choice made to learn or not to learn. Until the knowledge of choice is attained, the psyche is learning indirectly. The environment is shaping the psyche, yet, at the same time, the persona is conceptualizing Being in a particular setting. This same thing may be said of the mentally handicapped and even the mentally healthful, especially when the latter normally at times does not think of learning or set out to learn. However, the mentally healthful psyche begins to learn directly upon attaining the knowledge of choice. The persona here chooses to engage in the conflict of Being simulated in the environment. The environment or setting comprised of nature and society becomes, for the psyche, the fullness of all cosmic Being.

In the setting, energies of the psyche conflict with the counter energies of the setting. The persona is impressed with these energies. Perhaps this may be likened to one who experiences a multitude of tiny electric shocks about the size of pricks from needle points. These shocks or pains analogize negative impressions that result into positive images. For another illustration, one may consider the formation of the image on a coin, which also results from a negative impress. The form and substance of both mind and psyche are being shaped. Each of these resultant images (percepts) are by nature antithetical to one another. This is why the psyche does not comprehend all of them immediately. Yet, at the same time, the persona is synergizing these antitheses while energies of the psyche are conflicting with the counter energies of the setting, thereby, receiving impressions.

To synergize as the substance of Reconciliation means to bond or connect the antithesis (either-or) without losing the nature of its contrasts. This synergy depicts the struggle of the rational synthesis toward the ambivalence of the contrast (both-and). For example, the psyche that is learning directly is synthesizing immediate antithetical impressions (percepts) with the antithetical impressions of the past (percepts, concepts, ideas, and beliefs). The struggle of the persona in synergizing past and present exemplifies the psyche's struggle for wholeness of mind. Wholeness of mind is illustrated by the resultant successful sythesization of contrasts: the both-and paradox. In contrast, the psyche that does not choose to engage in conflict cannot attain wholeness of mind. In keeping with our example, the psyche does not totally synthesize immediate impressions with past impressions, i.e., images. This results in fragmented understanding which can ultimately lead to narrow-mindedness, prejudice, ignorance, and even neurosis and psychosis. The persona that refuses to engage in conflict is not coping, and rather than making sense of antitheses, the persona is making nonsense out of them. To this end, the psyche's life becomes reductio ad absurdum.

Synergy may also be illustrated with semantics. Let us look at the examples of the antitheses death/life and matter/spirit. Before total synergy takes place in the psyche, we note the either-or relationship of these contrasts, namely either death or life or vice versa, and either matter or spirit or vice versa. In the psyche, these relationships are merely coincidental. The personality of opposites is stressed over their relationships. Here a fragmented understanding of the paradox of life is depicted. On the other hand, total synergy is depicted in the both-and relationship. Both-and depicts the tension of unity within difference. "The meeting of opposites" is something essential to wholistic understanding.[13] We note this tension of unity within difference in the meeting of contrasts, namely both matter and spirit or vice versa and both death and life or vice versa. Furthermore the both-and relationship may be inferred in such expressions as the following: death is the other side of life or vice versa and spirit is the other side of matter or vice versa. The

13 Howard A. Slaate, *The Pertinence of the Paradox*. New York: Humanities Press, 1968, p. 5

both here is, of course, spirit and matter and life and death; where-as, the both-and is depicted by the synthesis, the other side of. The implication of both-and as synthesis, the other side of, complete the synergy, thereby conveying the complete understanding of the paradox.

Upon the basis of what was said, synergy may not denote the exactness of order and logic as we normally have understood them in the western world. Scholasticism was one of the many examples of western scholarship to rationalize the paradox. For the sake of this discussion, rationalization refers to the attempt to "smooth the paradox out" by means of logic and systemization. To rationalize the paradox was to separate understanding from reality. It was an attempt to terminate the conflict. We can rationalize and philoso-phize the conflict away, but in reality we cannot terminate it.

The need for order and logic is not rejected here, however. Or-der and logic reflect merely the energizing of paradoxes without negating the conflict of contrasts. In the logic of sequence—for ex-ample, the progression 1, 2, 3—order is depicted, but each term is not isolated. Rather conflict is still going on between factors. That is, conflict ensues between 1 and 2, 2 and 3, and among 1, 2, and 3. Consequently, 1 does not, exactly, progress to 2, nor does 2, exact-ly, progress to 3, nor can 1, exactly, be 1, or 2, exactly, 2, etc. Even 2 + 2 may not, exactly, = 4. Such order and logic is, in reality, the way sense is made out of contrasts. Order and logic, in reality, should preserve the paradox.

In discussing the synergizing of contrasts let us return to the example of the *past/present* antithesis. History and biography are shaped by the synergizing of past and present as demonstrated by the *both-and* paradox. The psychologist Henry Bergson has shown that "memory itself is a reiterated act of interpretation." That is, as "we remember the past, we reconstruct it in accordance with our present ideas of what is important and what is not"[14] As said earlier, the present images impressed struggle through a rational synthesis with past images, thereby bonding selective ideas of the

14 Berger, Op. cit., p. 96

present with selected ones of the past. Consequently, the synergizing of ideas of the past/present paradox gives form and substance to the biography of the psyche. The same principle may be applied to the psyche's history.

This dynamic is added to the form and substance of biography as biography synergizes with the formulated philosophy and knowledge of the psyche. The sociologist, Peter Berger depicts this philosophy and knowledge system as taking on meaning with the concept *Weltanschauung* or universal meaning system. That is, biography finds its location in the psyche's philosophy and knowledge system.[15] This is demonstrated by classic conversion experiences cited by Berger as depicted in "*Augustine's Confessions:*" and Newman's *Apologia Pro Vita Sua.*" The convert's previous life takes on a new meaning in the light of a present experience. All experiences and knowledge of past and present suddenly make sense. The life immediately takes on new direction. New hope is even seen for the future. This moment is described as providential, i.e., "when the mist" was "lifted from before his eyes."[16] Berger also sights the doctrine of Satori in Zen Buddhism, i.e., "...seeing things with new eyes."[17] The contrasts of past, present and future synergize in the biography and philosophy of the psyche.

Earlier we inferred that the psyche learns "moment by moment." The learning "moment" is a miniature conversion experience not necessarily noticed in the psyche. Each "moment" conflicting percepts are synergized into concepts, e.g., the old is synthesized into (transformed by) the new. The paradox takes on new meaning. The same may be said as concepts synergize to form beliefs or values, and as beliefs form systems of belief or philosophies. Belief systems are meaning systems, but when they synergize with biography they become universal meaning systems. This "conversion" or learning

15 Op. cit., p. 61.
16 Op. cit.
17 Op. cit., p. 62.

experience is overwhelmingly noticeable to the psyche because it has resulted from the clustering of multifarious direct and indirect learning experiences. This universal meaning system is one "that is capable of ordering (synergizing) the scattered data (percepts, concepts and beliefs) of one's biography, which the psyche finds "liberating and profoundly satisfying."[18] Berger further states that this perhaps "has its roots in a deep human need for order, purpose, and intelligibility."

All in all, we have noted that life in reality is comprised of conflicts or antitheses without which all Being would be a vacuum. The persona learns by synergizing within, these antitheses into paradoxes. Each encounter of the psyche is, therefore, a crisis experience, which must be synergized. That is, the ambivalence of the paradox is maintained by bonding its opposite poles without losing the character of its opposites. When this is accomplished, true learning has taken place because the conflict of reality is accepted and understood. One's learning results through engaging in conflicts. In turn, the crises of struggles through engaging result in the derivation of new meaning. Therefrom these create new crises conflicts resulting in newer and more complete meaning than before ad infinitum. Such crisis or conflict learning may be briefly illustrated with the Hegelian dialectic.

---

18 Peter L. Berger, *Invitation to Sociology: A Humanistic Perspective.* New York: Doubleday and Company, Inc., 1963, p. 63

Figure 3: Percepts, Concepts, Ideas, and Beliefs

Thesis $\rightarrow\leftarrow$ Antithesis $\rightarrow$ Synthesis

$X_1 \rightarrow\leftarrow X_2 \rightarrow X_{1+2}$

$Percept_1 \rightarrow\leftarrow Percept_2 \rightarrow Concept_{1+2}$

$Concept_1 \rightarrow\leftarrow Concept_2 \rightarrow Idea_{1+2}$

$Idea_1 \rightarrow Idea_2 \rightarrow Belief$ (Value, Assumption, Philosophy) $_{1+2}$

The process of reclaiming the self is one of reconciliation with meaning.

Tariq Ramadan

Chapter Three

Ramifications of Reconciliation

The Esthetic of Reconciliation

From the proposition we derive the following hypotheses relative to Cross's theory of lifelong learning.[19] Although based in education, the proposition depicts compatibility with counseling in that the following hypotheses reflect developmental psychology through the life span. Reflectively, the theory of Reconciliation through education and counseling demonstrates the following compatibilities:

The proposition is compatible with the humanistic theory of learning and counseling because it allows freedom for individual choice in the how and what the psyche learns.

It is compatible with self-directed learning in that Reconciliation allows for multifaceted learning and counseling approaches. These are in addition to resource personnel, materials, and equipment for the facilitating of learning with challenging and encouraging learning experiences.

---

19 Cross, Op. cit, p. . 220.

It is compatible with the developmental or phasic theory because phases and periods of development may be explained and applied in terms of Reconciliation in learning and counseling.

It is compatible with the discovery learning approach because Reconciliation allows for the psyche to learn by personal experience and curiosity. Counseling may facilitate learning by personal experience while enhancing curiosity.

It is compatible with lifelong learning of the psyche because of its emphasis on the fundamental importance of biography and autobiography in relation to learning.

The theory of Reconciliation allows for the facilitation of choice in the psyche with its end as creating a tapestry or composition of meaning. Conflict presents challenges that stir feelings and thoughts of chaos within the psyche and its context. Self and identity are shaped either unto despair or meaning. Counseling and education enter in with teaching and guidance of the psyche into positive knowledge of self and world and the assurance of self.

Irrespective of the subject matter applied, Reconciliation may apply to the edification of self and Being through the chaotic world of conflict. For instance, a flower may be studied and analyzed for its properties, but it must also be studied for its esthetic. Through counseling and education, Reconciliation may be applied to the edification of the psyche both cognitively and affectively. The flower may be applied wholly to synergize the heart and mind of the psyche and persona, thereby, opening within self and Being an understanding of self and world that is transformative. Within the being of psyche, the window is opened to choice that receives the wisdom of knowledge.

A young man enters my office. He is around 16 years of age. He conveys that he has had a bad day at school. He has been seeing me for counseling and drug testing for around six weeks. By this time, he is demonstrating confidence in and a strong sense of belonging in the counseling context. Through my elicitations, he shares having trouble with algebra, and concern about declining grades in that class. I then ask him to share some algebra problems with me. From his worksheet, we consider two equations. I take him online, showing how the problems are demonstrated. In this manner, I encourage the use of the computer toward the Reconciliation of opposites not only in math but in other subject matters as well. Also, algebra is depicted as the language of the human mind. We consider the logic and order of equations and their development in steps toward a conclusion.

Through therapy, I guide him into the esthetic of apparent contradictions of difference regarding their conveyance of symmetry, balance and proportion. From here, we enter into the realm of the affective domain, the area of the heart. The client becomes empowered by sharing his consternation with parental pressure to earn top grades. He, being articulate and intelligent, related to the affective meaning. Thereupon, we enter into a slow breathing exercise with our eyes shut. After a short period, I ease into guiding him into the quiet place of his Being where all "conflicting objects" seemingly converge to the point of rest. There he experiences the quietness and peace of balance and symmetry. Of course, in a previous session, I had taught him about breathing and listening to his breath attentively, and now, our time was running out, so through feedback, he shares the following. He conveys that he cannot change the way his parents think, yet he must take each hour and day as it comes and look for balance in self with them.

From Logotherapy, we learn that the client may find meaning in life, by being engaged in a wide spectrum of values. This client was taught to see, think and feel values affectively and cognitively in the context of his learning and home contexts. In this session, we apply Frankl's three approaches to values application in counseling converge. These are the creative, the longitudinal and the attitudinal.[20]

---

20 Tim LeBon, Viktor Frankl and Logotherapy, http://www.timlebon.com/

From the standpoint of Gestalt, the client perceives world in terms of self. At first, his perception is fragmented. He is unable to find connections synergizing his solving of algebra equations, his overall school expectations and his parental expectations. Being guided into the synergism of heart and mind, the client invests into finding the Gestalt of meaning.[21] He is empowered in the perceptual claim of ownership regarding the situation, and begins to move into positive and effective self-directedness.22[22] As the artist of self, he manages the multifaceted palate of his personality and worldview. He perceives the asymmetry of fragmentation and, thereby, enters into the symmetry of the whole.

The Spirituality of Reconciliation

From the standpoint of spirituality, the technique of mindfulness breathing is applied to the client regarding his needs and his strengths. His needs stemmed from his coerced desire to learn algebra in the context of his parental demand to succeed in school. With a strongly devalued sense of self-worth, the client is lost in the overwhelming context of parental demands linked with school expectations. Introspection with breathing opens the gate to the heart and mind allowing the perception of feelings and thoughts. The client is empowered with the vision of his strengths of intelligence and perceptiveness and is thereby able to synergize and transform the chaotic elements of his worldview. In this manner, client self-directedness is facilitated.[23] The client has begun to recapture his self-worth and self-value. These concepts and approaches to

---

frankl.htm (accessed December 22, 2014).
21 What is Gestalt Therapy? http://www.gestalt.lv/eng/therapy/what_is_gestalt_theory/ (accessed December 22, 2014).
22 Self-Directed Learning, http://www.selfdirectedlearning.com/teaching-self-directed-learning-tools/articles/a-new-theory.html (accessed December 22, 2014)
23 Facilitating learning and change, http://infed.org/mobi/facilitating-learning-and-change-in-groups-and-group-sessions/ (accessed December 22, 2014); Instructional_Design: Facilitation Theory, http://teorije-ucenja.zesoi.fer.hr/doku.php?id=instructional_design:facilitation_theory (accessed December 22, 2014); The Person Centered Approach, http://www.bapca.org.uk/about/carl-rogers.htm (accessed December 22, 2014).

the person-centered therapy applied by Rogers to education are here being reapplied to therapy. [24]

Although Rogers takes a humanistic approach, in reality his approach is one of spirituality. He places a very high value on the human being. This value is what Maslow may term Meta in terms of value and Being. From a Biblical standpoint, human being reflects the image of God. The person of human being is rational, volitional, thinking and feeling, intelligent, with sensibilities of personability, caringness, lovingness, compassion, creativity, the philosophical, artistic, intuitive and scientific. No other creation of God is endowed with these faculties. Rogers and other humanistic psychologists, philosophers and educators respect these qualities in human beings, and, therefore, design theories based on these. Abraham Maslow speaks of B-values, namely, the values rising above the hierarchy of the values and needs of humankind. At the very base of the hierarchy of Being, man must meet animal needs, such as those of food, water, shelter and sex; however, on the very highest level of hierarchy, he reaches for the Meta or spiritual dimension. [25]

The therapeutic approach taken with this client assumes his engagement in life long development and learning. Hence, Reconciliation of the client with his challenges considers the science of adult education. That is, androgogy may be applied to the growing child and adolescent into adult years. Unlike contemporary pedagogy, andragogy focuses on the learning behavior and development of the student and client. In light of humanistic counseling and psychological theory, such an approach lends itself to counseling as well as teaching. Also, in light of androgiogical science, mathetics explains learning behavior while pedagogy explains teacher behavior in the learning of pupils. Although this was not the ancient approach of the pedagogue, pedagogy was inclusive of both

24 Person-Centered Therapy, http://en.wikipedia.org/wiki/Person-centered_ therapy (accessed December 22, 2014)
25 Frank G. Goble, *The Third Force: Psychology of Abraham Maslow*. New York: Grossman Publishers, 1970, p. 50 cf. Abraham H. Maslow, *Religions, Values, and Peak-Experiences*. New York: The Viking Press, 1964.

teacher and disciple. Today, however, the substance of both androgogy and mathetics focuses upon learning behavior from childhood through adult years while androgogy focuses upon learning
in adulthood. Both sciences depict the original role of the pedagogue. Concomitantly, they involve the probabilities, the possibilities, and the why and how of lifelong learning.[26]

Because the human being is substantially spiritual, volitional,
humane and rational, clients and students are endowed with the
predisposition toward self-directability. They need only motivation, guidance, interest and talent. In this light, the counseling
context along with the approach of mathetics and androgogy assumes the aforementioned humanistic traits as natural to the development and learning of clients and students.

Development and Maturation in Reconciliation

In the counseling context, the client is highly valued as a learner
in the developmental process of life. This psyche is acquiring cognitive and affective development relative to conceptual formation
and values formation in experiential contexts. Through the facilitation of self-reflection and self-interaction, the client is moved
toward the increasing of choices relative to acquiring knowledge
and decision-making skills leading toward the synergy of opposites. As with lifelong education, a creative and wholistic approach
to counseling, considers the development of the psyche from conception through the senior years.

The adult theory and approach to education, as being applied to
adolescent and young adult students and clients effectively, is substantiated in the following findings. Bornstein and Kessen pointed
out that whereas psychologists such as William James "were prone
to characterize the infant's world as a 'blooming, buzzing confusion,' contemporary developmental investigators find instead dis-

---

26 J. R. Kidd, *How Adults Learn,* New York: Association Press, 1973,
p. 23 cf. Malcolm S. Knowles, *The Modern Practice of Adult Education: Androgogy Versus Pedagogy,* New York: Association Press, 1970;
Malcolm S. Knowles, *The Adult Learner:* A Neglected Species, 1978;
Cross, Op. cit.,

cerning responses to complex visual and auditory displays." As observed in adults, infants' "functions include frequent discrimination and speech categorization as well as luminance discrimi

nation and hue categorization. A close look at infantile perception reveals foundations of and parallels with mature behavior."[27]

During the prenatal period, fetal "mass activity" is noted prior to the third prenatal month. During that month, however, "mass activity becomes spontaneous" in that such activity is no longer dependent on "external stimuli." As time goes on, "mass activity" becomes increasingly differentiated, "thus allowing different parts of the body to move independently of the rest of the body" [28] Also, the fetus begins to respond differentially to its environment and will icon the varied emotions of the mother. These behaviors convey evidence that infants do begin to learn before birth as well as after birth. However, much of knowledge regarding prenatal learning still lies in the realm of speculation and fragmentation. Nevertheless, cognitive and affective development iconing mature adults is observed postnatally; whereas, affective development is first observed prenatally.[29]

Hurlock points out that such development is dependent on maturation and learning. Both are interrelated with the former being "the unfolding of traits inherent in the individual" and the latter being the act of "'each organism...permitting itself to be modified by selected aspects of its immediate environment.'" In turn, maturation provides the raw material for learning and determines the more general patterns and sequences of the individual's behavior."[30]

27 Mare H. Bornstein and William Kessen (Eds.), *Psychological Development from Infancy: Image to Intention.* New York: John Wiley and Sons, 1979, p. 46.
28 Elizabeth B. Hurlock, *Developmental Psychology.* New York: McGraw-Hill Book Company, 1968, p. 72
29 Hurlock Op. cit., p. 72 cf. Bornstein and Kessen (Eds.) Op. cit.; Edward C. Carterette, and Morton P. Friedman (Eds.), *Handbook of Perception: Historical and Philosophical Roots of Perception.* New York: Academic Press, I, 1974
30 Hurlock, Op cit., pp. 19-20. .

Reconciliation depicts the psyche as engaged in conflict "moment by moment." Points of resolution with self and opposites result in the synergizing of self with opposites in context and psyche. Knowles points out that much research regarding the "teachable moment" has been undertaken regarding children, e.g., Hurlock's studies. Yet he also unveils that recent research "suggests the same phenomenon at work through [adolescent and] adult years. [Adolescents and] adults, too, have their phases of growth and resulting developmental tasks, readiness to learn, and teachable moments.[31]

Reconciliation along with the data of this study assumes the adolescent psyche in the context of child and adult learning and development. Self-direction and trust is applied to the adolescent psyche through the approach of Reconciliation and conflict. Reconciliation assumes the natural need of adolescents as well as children and adults for trust, decision-making and self-direction, and essential to these is the substance of creativity and spirituality in the human psyche.

Bruner informs us, although he is thinking in the light of symbolic representation during childhood learning development, as cited: "growth is characterized by increasing independence of response from the immediate nature of the stimulus."[32] The young child responds to the stimulus by direct imitation, but as the psyche matures, the persona internalizes a "storage system" (what I call a meaning system) corresponding to the environment (setting), which gives the maturing child an "increasing ability to go beyond the information encountered on a single occasion" [33]

As the child becomes an adult, the storage system increases to a universal meaning system or sets of universal meaning systems that separate the psyche even more so from stimuli. Prenatally and postnatally (even into the toddler years), the child's learning experiences minus the motivation of curiosity may be explained in

31 Knowles, Op. cit., 1970, p. 46.
32 Brunner, Op. cit., p. 5.
33 Op cit. cf. Robert F. Biehler, *Psychology Applied to Teaching*. Boston: Houghton Mifflin Company, 1974.

terms of the S-R formula—that is, the direct stimulus elicits a direct response. Yet on into later childhood, adolescence and adulthood, the S-R mechanism gives way to the S-O-R function or schema. O is equal to the "intervening variable;" O denotes "the person... the one stimulated and the one responding," and fundamental to the person's learning behavior are the covert meaning systems and universal meaning systems which again are the equivalent of Bruner's internalized "storage system." McClusky points out that as the psyche matures "perception is highly selective." That is to say, "part of stimulation which finally becomes a part of experience is NOT a random sample of what is totally available" [quite a contrast to early childhood). "There is (a) selective exposure within the exposure field, [and] (b) selective awareness." Hence, the maturing psyche is unaware of all sensory experiences.[34]

Nevertheless, "a person perceives things in patterns that are meaningful to him."[35] This certainly supports our discussion regarding the past/present antithesis. That is, as we remember past experiences, we synergize them with present experiences.[36] This theory is also related to Gestalt theory, which indicates that the psyche builds meaningful wholes ("patterns or configurations") by means of "organizing bits and pieces of information." These percepts or concepts denote figures that become comprehensible in a context of ground. For example, the parts that comprise a tree are perceived and synergized as tree. The psyche relates each part to the other and its background or environment.[37] The meaning system or concept(s) of tree are then stored into Bruner's "storage system. "[38]

Also, for the maturing psyche, percepts themselves do not represent an exact "interpretation of what is perceived" but "are clearly influenced by the needs, disposition and set which a person brings

34 McClusky in Knowles, Op cit., 1970, pp. 150-151 cf. Brunner, Op. cit.
35 Op cit., p. 151
36 Bergson in Berger, Op cit., p. 56
37 Mary Lou Ginsberg, Kenneth Henry, and Dennis Krebs, *Understanding Psychology*, Second Edition. New York: Random House, Inc., 1977 cf. Brunner, Jerome, Op cit., p. 5.
38 Brunner, Op cit., p. 5.

to the perceptual experience." For example, " in a classic experiment Bruner and Postman demonstrated that in the case of ten-year-old boys the perception of the size of coins was directly related not to size but the value (to the boys) [O] of the coin." Therefore, the individual's perception of the stimulus (S) rather than the "raw physical property of the stimulus" becomes the knowledge (O) that will elicit a response [R] accordingly. McClusky further illus trates this with two following antitheses: "Hence, I know [O] What [S] I say [R] but I do not know[-O] what [-S] you hear [-R];I may know[O] what [S]I show [R] but I do not know [-O] what [-S] you see [-R]."[39]

Perhaps McClusky has cited the essence of Questioning—the characteristic of adolescence. Henry cites the adolescent as being concerned about age-old questions such as the following:

'What is man? Whence does he come from and whither does he go? Why should the righteous suffer? Are all our human strivings and ideals part of some greater plan, or are they just an accident on a tiny bit of cosmic dust? What is worth living for? What is worth dying for?'[40]

The adolescent, unlike the child, questions in the abstract. The adolescent psyche has moved away from the mimesis of the child. The adolescent psyche in the ancient world, and in many of Near and Middle Eastern cultures of today becomes a man or a woman at the ages of twelve to fourteen years. In Greco-Roman and early Hebraic cultures, the child remained under the care of a tutor (paidogogos: child/boy leader, derived from the Greek pais, paidos and ago) in the "father's" household until "he" became a "man" (anir, andros, 'o).[41] An andros demonstrated the characteristics physically and psychologically of a contemporary adolescent. The questioning adolescent was now individuated to the point that

39 McClusky in Knowles, Op cit., 1970, pp. 151-152
40 Virgil Henry, *The Place of Religion in Public Schools: A Handbook to Guide Communities*. New York: Harper and Brothers Publishers, 1950, p.21
41 Arndt and Goodrich, Op. cit., 1957

"he" could now "put away childish things" (1 Corinthians 13:11). At this point, through a ceremonial rite of passage, e.g., Roman citizenship or Jewish Bar Mitzvah, the paidos gave way to the andros.

This is an anthropological explanation of Knowles' concept of androgogy.[42] That is, the child's learning is characteristically based on mimesis (concrete imitation); whereas, the maturing adolescent and adult learns through experiences in the context of "social roles."[43] The meaning system of adolescent and adult is highly integrated with these experiences, and "moment by moment" the both are ever increasingly separated from "raw stimuli" (S) by a vast range of experiences and knowledge (O). Hence, the adult and adolescent develop an individuation that is self-directing.

Mimesis is well illustrated by Rene' Girard in his anthropological work, Violence and the Sacred (1977). He points out that violence, for example, was learned by a child imitating a teacher. Mimesis was the characteristic-learning trait of primitive societies, but as societies matured they developed a system of religion through the sacrifice of the surrogate victim to cloak and deflect violence. This way, the society was ordered and preserved from the danger of mimetic violence. This system of religion is likened to the knowledge or universal meaning system of the contemporary adult psyche. Again this knowledge individuates adolescent and adult by separating the psyche from cognitive and affective dependence on the environment as demonstrated by the prenatal fetus and the postnatal infant. Hence, as the newly citizenized Roman or Bar Mitzvahed Jew, the adult male is permitted to become self-directed. [44]

Now the question is posed: at what point should the paidos give

---

42 Knowles, Op cit., 1970; Op cit., 1978
43 Op cit., 1970, p. 46
44 Michael Grant, *The World of Rome*. New York, World Publishing Company, 1960; History of Bar Mitzvah, http://www.myjewishlearning. com/life/Life_Events/BarBat_Mitzvah/History/Bar_Mitzvah.shtml (accessed December 27, 2014); Israel, Abrahams, et al., *Jewish Values*. Jerusalem, Israel: Keter Publishing House Jerusalem, Ltd., 1974

way to the andros in society today? In ancient societies discussed, the rite of passage was the line of demarcation, but today it is not as simple. We note that adolescents physically, intellectually, and psychologically are at the point of becoming self-directed, yet they are caught in the tension of their newly perceived individuation and the socialization of a highly complex society. Resultantly, they are restrained from the individual they naturally sense. The creative urge of self-direction gives then the strong since of readiness for self-reliance and autonomy. Once children reach puberty, we should facilitate their maturation in increasingly independent roles through educational experiences. Such an approach is substantiated by Knowles.[45] His conclusions are summarized in the following: "as an individual matures, his need and capacity to be self-directing, to utilize his experience in learning, to identify his own readiness to learn, and to organize his learning around life's problems, increases steadily from infancy to preadolescence, and then increases rapidly during adolescence" [Italics mine].[46]

Knowles posits a gradual increase in motivation as dependency decreases. That is, children in the first year of school are dependent on pedagogy, namely the teacher approach to learning in students, but from the second grade on pedagogy becomes decreasingly appropriate. Nevertheless, Knowles indicates that "American culture (home, school, religious institutions, youth agencies, governmental systems) assumes—and therefore permits –a growth rate" among growing children and adolescents that is much slower than their developmental and maturation levels. [47] Reflectively, culture and education do not "nurture the development of abilities required for creativity and self-direction while the need to be increasingly self-directing continues to develop organically. The result manifests a growing gap between the need and the ability to be self-directing, and this produces tension, resistance, resentment, and often rebellion in the individual."[48] The inability of education and culture to

45 Knowles, Op. cit., 1970, p. 54
46 Op cit..
47 Knowles, Op cit., 1978, p. 55
48 Op cit

fill this learning gap in growing children and adolescents results in ever increasing behavior and learning problems in school and society. Teacher centered education should gradually be phased out with client and student centered education and counseling as indicated by theorists and research discussed thus far.

The whole difference between construction and creation is exactly this: that a thing constructed can only be loved after it is constructed; but a thing created is loved before it exists.

Charles Dickens

Chapter Four

Individuation and Reconciliation

Individuation in Reconciliation

Crucial to learning and maturation in this discussion is the nature of individuation in the psyche. Choice compels individuation and, at the same time, Reconciliation gives primacy to choice as the first cause of learning. In turn, learning enhances the function of choice. We also noted that as the meaning system (stored learning) increases, the psyche is gradually growing detached from the environment. This is the essence of McClusky's S-O-R theory. The instatement of O between S and R is the "indispensible factor in understanding and influencing the learning process." S and R being "anchored in" the learning psyche "is especially relevant in the adult years when experience becomes [increasingly] cumulative and behavior increasingly differentiated." [49]

Increasing differentiation denotes the increase of choice with knowledge through the reflexive action between choice and the increasing of the meaning system within the psyche. McClusky's antitheses, e.g., "...I know [O] what [S] I say [R] but I do not know [-O] what [-S] you hear [-R]..." demonstrates the ability of the psyche to discriminate and differentiate stimuli and to relate it to its meaning system and its ability not to discriminate and differen-

49 Knowles, Op cit., 1978, p. 55

tiate. This latter negative concept may be explained in terms of either a lack of awareness, forgetfulness, or overlooking. In contrast, the former positive concept may be explained in terms of what is intentionally perceived and what is intentionally rejected. [50]

Figure 4: Negative and Positive Learning and Storage

$$\overset{=}{X} = \begin{vmatrix} X = (S <\text{-}> O \text{-}> R) \\ -X = -(S <\text{-}> O \text{-}> R) \end{vmatrix}$$

Consequently, the derived equation, being imperfect, attempts to summarize each learning moment of the individuating adolescent and adult psyche. X denotes the total knowledge synergized as a result of both equations. The first equation [x= (S→←O→R)] , represents the reflexive action between stimuli (S) and the psyche (O) which, in turn, is an attempt to denote the tension of conflict between S and O and the discriminating function of O. x is equal to this total learning behavior of the psyche. The second equation [-x = - (S→←O →R)] demonstrates the same reflexive action, but learning experiences are rejected by the psyche [-O] through negative storage via discrimination, forgetfulness and unawareness. The X is the result of composite learning behavior summed up in both x and –x. However, x and –x must exist side by side as an antithesis. To total them would cancel out X; thus, for the sake of Reconciliation, the final result is X = [x, -x]. In this manner, Reconciliation indicates the psyche as always learning (engaged in conflict) regardless of the choice to learn or not to learn. Choice remains dominant in the learning process, directly and indirectly.

Relative to choice is the process of individuation. The psyche from conception through the stages of development increases choice and awareness of self through conflict.[51] The ego denotes

50 Op cit
51 The process of individuation, http://www.soul-guidance.com/

the organization of the conscious mind with functions of perceiving, thinking, remembering and feeling, which, in turn, bring the psyche to a state of awareness. The function of the psyche is to be "highly selective" in its shaping of the personality. The free will (choice function) is dependent on consciousness, and consciousness, in turn, is increased through experiences that the ego channels into the consciousness. Essentially, increased consciousness results from learning, which is synonymous with heightened awareness. With increased consciousness, choice is increased, and, therefore, individuation. With Jung, the function of choice must always presuppose consciousness.[52]

Hence, we consider the stream of consciousness. William James describes this concept in terms of "four important characters:"

• Every 'state' tends to be part of a personal consciousness. This 'state' refers to one's experiential reality cognitively or affectively in any situation at a given place and time.
• Within each personal consciousness states are always changing.
• Each personal consciousness is sensibly continuous.
• It is interested in some parts of its object to the exclusion of others, and welcomes or rejects—chooses from among them, in a word—all the while. [53]

In essence, James believes that the consciousness learns by the choice functions of "accentuation and emphasis." These functions "are present in every perception we have." For example, "a monotonous succession of sonorous strokes is broken up into rhythms, now of one sort, now of another, by the different accent which we place on different strokes. The simplest of these rhythms is the double one, tick-tock, tick-tock, tick-tock." Also, "the ubiquity of

houseofthesun/individuationprocess.htm (accessed December 28, 2014)
52 Calvin S. Hall and Vernon J. Nordby, *A Primer of Jungian Psychology*. New York: The New American Library, 1973 cf. *The Structure and Dynamics of the Psyche. The Collected Works of C. G. Jung:* Sir Robert Read, et al. (Eds.). London: Routledge and Kegan Paul, 1960, pp. 8:3-66.
53 James, Op. cit., 1963, p. 147.

the distinctions, this and that, here and there, now and then, in our minds is the result of our laying the same selective emphasis on parts of place and time." "Attention, on the other hand, [a function of the conscious in relation to choice] out of all the sensations yielded, picks out certain ones as worthy of notice and suppresses all the rest."[54]

With James, one's choice may infer attention; whereas, lack of choice may infer inattention. Objects of attention pass through the consciousness, yet objects of inattention pass through the unconsciousness. Through Reconciliation objects of attention and inattention are processed differently in terms of time and approach. They may be synergized immediately while others are synergized over time. Many objects of consciousness and unconsciousness are stored in McClusky's storage system, O. We here infer a stream of unconsciousness complementing the stream of consciousness.

The aforementioned theorists describe learning and development in terms of choice using varied metaphors and approaches, but all seem to agree with choice as the principle mechanism in learning and development. The end of education in this study is to facilitate the creative energy of the psyche through choice. Along with this comes interest and desire. We assume that learning must be self-directed through a strong individualized and discovery orientation. The teacher becomes a facilitator with genuine positive regard for the student. Likewise the counselor takes the same approach with the student as client. The counselor strives to support the cognitive and affective learning development of the client by focusing upon the client's needs, strengths, abilities, interests and talents. At the same time, teacher and counselor remain in concert with the learning and developmental process of the psyche.

Corroborating this wholistic approach to facilitating choice and creativity in counseling and education also reflects the approach of Rollo May. As an Existentialist, he teaches that human behavior is based on one's choice among alternatives. His belief that the

---

54 Op. cit., pp. 161-163

psyche is "Being-in-the world" presupposes a psychology of consciousness in which both consciousness and choice are fundamental to freedom from alienation from the world.[55] Consequently, May believes that one learns through consciousness and choice. He teaches that choice in perception and conception is exercised through intention. By turning one's (subjective) attention toward something (objective), both subject and object act upon one another, thereby, shaping one another through the media of intention and attention. May writes: "If we take the time-honored metaphor of the sculptor and his clay, we must see the clay also forms the sculptor; the clay conditions what he does, limits and even changes his intentions, and, thus, also forms his intentions, and thus, also forms his potentialities and consciousness."[56]

All in all, the dialectics of fundamental concept building and learning takes place around choice. We have noted the dialectic (reflexive) between choice (CH) and concept formation, i.e., meaning system (M) results in consciousness (CN). Here the persona is developed as the psyche (O) is engaged in conflict within the seeing $(S \rightarrow \leftarrow O \rightarrow R)$. This is illustrated in the following: $CH \rightarrow \leftarrow CN \rightarrow M$.

As said earlier, the psyche comprises the total learning behavior (life) of the persona, which becomes increasingly individuated through each learning "moment." With Jung, however, the learning mechanism of the psyche indicates the reflexive between consciousness (CN) and knowledge (K or M) resulting in the shaping of choice in the ego. Note the illustration as follows: K-M??CN?CH.

With James and May we have the following dialectic. This is taking place between consciousness (CN) and (CH) resulting in meaning (M-K): $CN \rightarrow \leftarrow CH \rightarrow M$.

---

55 George Fuller, James Calhoun, and Martin Schulman, *Understanding Psychology*, Second Edition. New York: Random House, Inc. 1977; Chaplin, James P. and T. S. Krawiec, *Systems and Theories of Psychology*, Third Edition. New York: Holt, Rinehart and Winston, Inc., 1974
56 Rollo May, *Love and Will*. New York: W. W. Norton and Company, Inc., 1969, p. 235

Individuation and Cognitive Dissonance
in Reconciliation

In conjunction with this discussion, Rogers explains the learning and motivation of the psyche in terms of organism and self. Roger's organism is somewhat close to our understanding of persona and self in that organism is the location of awareness yet like the psyche, the organism reflects the totality of experience constituting the phenomenal field of Beingness and the frame of reference of the person and self, i.e., the persona. In this study, we need to repeat the persona, as the personality of the psyche to which is attributed mind, heart and consciousness. The personality also includes presentation of self and psyche to others.[57]

In the classical and New Testament Greek, the equivalent of psyche (psyche) denoted one's life on earth.[58] This life is the total equivalent of the dynamics of the human being in a respective environment. On the other hand, the persona (Latin for "role, part, character, or person represented by an actor"), Being centered on choice and meaning denotes the developing and maturing psyche.[59] This is somewhat equivalent to Roger's self, which "is an organized and consistent whole; though constantly changing, it is specific at any moment."[60]

Rogers also adds that every organism has an ideal self—that person he or she would like to become. Learning takes place between self and ideal self. As Rogers found out through client centered therapy, this dissonance can also be threatening and abrasive, thereby compelling the person to "take various unhealthful ways of relieving the tension." Rogers also teaches that conflicts arise from the environment, "especially the social environment: between the self and organism, because both of these factors "possess strong

---

57 Kidd, Op. cit., p. 127
58 Arndt and Gingrich, Op. cit.
59 Simpson, 1959
60 Kidd, Op. cit., p. 127

tendencies to actualize." The organism in its respective environment also learns by the dissonance of self and organism as well as self and ideal self. The conflicts of dissonance demonstrated here would definitely be related to the development of choice, meaning system and consciousness—these principle factors in the process of individuation.[61]

---

61 Op. cit. cf. Rogers, Op. cit. 1961; Fuller, Calhoun, and Schulman, Op. cit.

The worst mistake you can make with children is to talk to them in a condescending, patronising way and think that you can teach them something. You have to understand that it is you who will be learning from them. You have to get into their world and see things from their perspective.

Magnus Scheving

Chapter Five

Reconciliation and Development

Adult and Adolescent Learning Distinctions

Throughout this study, the writer has been focusing on (1) the covert learning process of the psyche, (2) the engendering of this learning process through interaction with self and environment, and (3) the learning process and its impact upon maturation and development, which is equated with individuation and intellectual development. Of course, in this study, time cannot be given to all the factors of psyche development and growth through interrelations with the learning process. Unfortunately time cannot even be spent in giving details of learning relative to every proven stage and developmental phase of the human organism. Nevertheless, time is being given to the intellectual (cognitive and affective) development of the psyche through Reconciliation. We have noted the transition of individuation from childhood to adulthood via the adolescent stage of abstract thinking (e.g., the formal operational stage 11 years of age and above).[62]

In Piaget's model, the characteristics of adolescent intellectual processes do carry over and remain in the adult years. Adults, like adolescents, do think in terms of possibilities and are "capable of imagining various future alternative and developing hypotheses."[63]

---

62 Piaget in Biehler, 1974, p. 118
63 Op. cit.

Adults, on the other hand, apply their intellectual processes (already discussed) to immediate reality as well as future reality. We also noted this transition in light of adult education theory and anthropological illustrations. Also, in the discussion of pedagogy phasing away to androgogy, the attempt was made to begin a model for lifelong education in relation to the theory and approaches to learning and counseling through Reconciliation.

My understanding that adults apply their intellectual processes to immediate reality as well as future reality is in keeping with Knowles' conclusion that "the adult years are the products primarily of the evolution of social roles."[64] Havinghurst "divides the adult years into three phases—'early adulthood (18-30), middle age (30-50) and later maturity (55 and over)—and identifies ten social roles of adulthood: worker, mate, parent homemaker, son or daughter of aging parents, citizen, friend, organization member, religious affiliate, and user of leisure time."[65] As adults move through these three phases, the requirements of their social roles change. Both Allport and Rogers help us to understand that the self (persona) goes through many phases in the context of each changing social role. Kidd cites at least four different "aspects of self" that take place during a major or minor "crisis of identity."[66] These are as follows: "What the person actually does and says, how the person perceives and feels his own behavior, what the person does as perceived by others, [and] the ideal self (in Freudian theory the superego) which each of us carries, constant while constantly changing, throughout life"[67]

Here the writer is submitting the idea of conflicts of identity to describe the minor crises that each of us faces in the context of our own roles. Unlike the contemporary adolescent, adults must cope with reality as they carry on their daily duties of livelihood, for the adult, unlike the adolescent, is responsible for the self and other,

---

64 Knowles, Op. cit., p. 46
65 Op. cit.
66Kidd, Op. cit., p. 126
67 Op. cit.

i.e., the family. As the adult must be economically independent, the adolescent is still dependent on the adult, viz., the parent or guardian. On the other hand, in Greco-Roman society, the adolescent who on one day was a child took on the office and responsibilities of andros through a rite of passage the next day. Consequently, the adolescent of ancient society, like today's adult, had to think both abstractly and concretely in the context of immediate and future realities.

Intellectual and Psychological
Developmental Stage Theories

Although Havinghurst and others have cited ages for phasic and developmental stages, one would find difficulty identifying intellectual development in terms of physical age.[68] Piaget pointed out "cognition in a given person is likely to involve a mixture of [intellectual] stages, according to how thoroughly the highest stage reached has been mastered."[69] Cropley further points out "the basic mechanism that permits development to occur is twofold, involving the capacity to relate new experience to existing cognitive structures on the one hand (assimilation), and the capacity to adapt existing structures to mismatches with environmental inputs, on the other (accommodation)."[70] At this point, one may add that even though Piaget's developmental psychology does have a strong biological orientation it allows for "inter-personal differences in cognitive function, according to the particular patterns of interaction between different individuals and their environments."[71] This would even include "different degrees of cognitive development and different levels of ability to sustain higher-level cognitive functioning" during "stressful conditions" through

---

68 Op. cit. pp. 126-127
69 A. J. Cropley, *Lifelong Education*: A Psychological Analysis. New York: Pergamon Press, 1977, p. 88 cf. Stage Theory of Cognitive Development, http://www.learning-theories.com/piagets-stage-theory-of-cognitive-development.html (accessed January 03, 2014)
70 Op. cit
71 Op. cit

"different patterns of experiences" within changing social roles and phases.[72]

For the sake of this discussion, let us review Piaget's theory of intellectual development. During the sensorimotor states (birth-2 years) the human organism learns "about properties of things through senses and motor activity."[73] Op. cit Upon moving into the preoperational stage (2-7 years), the human organism acquires the ability to manipulate "symbols and objects." The language acquisition factor of the psyche is "egocentric," denoting the thinking of one word at a time and environmental detachment in thinking. Eventually, the psyche thinks "of more than one quality at a time" (decenters) and begins to converse and understand conversation. During the concrete operational stage (7-11 years), the psyche is able to "conserve, decenter, and reverse but only with reference to concrete objects." This is accomplished through mental manipulation. The psyche also acquires the ability "to deal with operations—interiorized actions involving reversibility—but no ability to generalize beyond actual experience." The final stage, the formal operational (11 years and over), is indicated, of course, by the psyche's ability to deal with the abstract as well as the concrete.

Overview: Stages of Learning through Life

With respect to the process of learning, the prenatal stage may be described through the simple S-R formula. The maturing and growing fetus is subject to respond only to the physical and emotional stimuli of the mother. The conflict it experiences is indirectly received through the mother. During the sensorimotor stage the psyche moves from S-R learning to simple S-O-R learning. The psyche is still dependent on responding directly to stimuli in the environment and simple conflict in learning. The latter is indicated through the psyche's "eventual development of new ways of dealing with situations." Beginning with the preoper-

---

72 Op. cit
73 Op. cit. cf. Biehler, Op. cit., p. 118

ational and on through the formal operational stages the dialectic of learning grows more complex. At this point, it is proper to describe the learning process as: $(S \rightarrow \leftarrow O \rightarrow R)$. During the period of the formal operational stage from adolescence through the adult years (S??O?R) may be explained through the Hegelian dialectic $(X_1 \rightarrow \leftarrow X_2 \rightarrow X_{1+2})$ because of the complexity of the learning process demonstrated in Reconciliation theory.[74]

Of course, the evolution of the learning mechanism (discussed earlier) is indicated in the unfolding individuation and self-direction of the psyche. The point here is that the intellectual (cognitive and affective) processes continue to grow throughout the life of the psyche, including the adult years unless extreme deterioration of the body through certain diseases occur. At the same time, adults in their 40's and 50's learn slower than those in their 20's and 30's, not because they are losing intelligence, but because learning speed is gradually slowing down. Cross writes that "speed of learning involves reaction time to perceive the stimulus, transmission time to transmit the message to the brain, and response time to carryout the action."[75] On the average, "older learners (those 40 and above) perceive more slowly, think more slowly, and act more slowly than younger people;" thus the "time required for learning new things increases with age."[76]

Although reaction time does slow down, familiarity with learning tasks gives the older person a chance to pace learning activity. Even though speed of learning does vary from person to person, slowness in learning results from the complexity of the learning task. Also, the thinking processes of older people are much more complex than that of younger people, e.g., adolescents, because they have highly varied and complex experiences to relate with including past and present responsibilities and experiences. This should also be understood in light of the fact that the older psyche

---

74 cf. Cross, Op. cit., Knowles, Op. cit., Piaget in Biehler, Op. cit., Piaget in Cropley, 1979, Stage Theory of Cognitive Development, Op. cit.
75 Cross, Op. cit., p. 155
76 Cross, Op. cit.,

has interiorized a more complex meaning system than the younger psyche (especially the adolescent) and will, therefore, perceive and conceive in greater detail. On may conclude here that adults learn in terms of quality; whereas, their younger counterparts learn in terms of quantity.

Chapter Six

The Adult and Reconciliation

Characteristics of Adulthood

In the United States, commonly when we think of aging, we think of "the problem" of growing old. However, gerontologists have concluded, "defining the 'older person' is no easy task." Aging is a gradual process that takes place throughout life, and 'biologists agree that almost as soon as the [human] organism stops growing it begins the process of growing old." Customarily, people have identified old age with the "seventh decade of life," but we now recognize "that the real turning point comes much earlier."[77]

Consequently, these stages of "advanced adulthood" have been defined. These are "middle age, later maturity, and old age." Although the time frames are cited as follows, since the date of these citations, these time frames have seemingly advanced three to five years. Nevertheless, characteristics of middle age (from ~45 through ~55 years) are noted. The psyche senses the experience of advancing in age with slower response times. Illness tends to increase with the experience of chronic diseases in the bodily organs. The senses begin to diminish along with memory. In the face of all of this, death becomes an impending reality. At the same time, environmental factors begin to change engendering major adjust-

---

77 Robert C. Atchley, *The Social Forces in Later Life: An Introduction to Social Gerontology.* Belmont, California: Wadsworth Publishing Company, 1972, pp. 6-8 cf.

ment issues to the absence of children in the home, the probability of impending retirement, while having to face a sense of goalessness for self, career and family. [78]

Characteristics of later maturity (~55 through ~65 years of age) are "marked by" the following. The confrontation with impending death increases. Diseases increase with frequent visits to the physician's office and increased surgeries. Friends, family members and acquaintances begin to experience terminal illnesses and death. Widowhood most likely looms or happens. Also, the psyche is either on the brink of retirement or dealing with the struggle of dreams and goals most likely being unrealized. Income is reduced along with the potential for activity and involvements. Such a person then finds the self, struggling with greater time and not knowing what to do with it. Although energy is waning, the psyche most likely strives for health, vigor and vitality. [79]

Last of all, old age (~65 and over) most likely is demonstrated by the following characteristics. If the psyche is unable to maintain a modicum of healthfulness, the person can experience symptoms of dementia and major declining of neural responses. In fact, he or she may likely experience the following: (1) "the slowing down of mental processes; (2) frailty, disability, or invalidism; (3) awareness that the end is very near; activity being greatly restricted; and (4) the commonness of "loneliness and boredom."[80]

At this point, we note that in contrast to the phases of "old age," "people in their early thirties are characteristically fixated on 'making it' in the world of work." They are also concerned with making a home and rearing their children. Around ages 37 through 45, adults usually encounter the need for that crucial promotion on the job helping then settle into their work. They are still confronted with growing children and usually become newly confronted

---

78 Op. cit.
79 Op. cit.
80 Op. cit.

with aging parents. Then around ages 45 through 55, they are able to settle down and rest in their careers. At this point, they begin to develop new interests as their children begin to gradually leave home to take on their own career and familial responsibilities.[81]

Age and Identity Crises

Each of these characteristics including physical, social and cultural changes impact upon Roger's self and Loevenger's ego, thereby, engendering a state of flux or dissonance within the human organism. Consequently, the self or ego is caught in the tension of dissonance between ideal self and true self, and possibly in really severe cases, it may even be caught between the dissonance of true self and organism. If caught in the dissonance of all these, an identity crisis may result in the psyche's view of self (self-esteem). An identity crisis may result when the older person in American culture finds the self as rejected due to age. Resultantly, the individual is not able "to achieve a satisfactory identity" in such a new position.[82]

Motivation and Change

The germ of these findings regarding the processes of the human life cycle is that of change. Gross writes that adults "have a fuller, richer, more stable and autonomous sense of self than children do, and a repertoire of experiences from which to draw as they read, discuss, create, and experiment."[83] Whereas, children learn under the guidance of a pedagogue, adults through self-direction sense an urgency to learn what they need in the present "because of all

---

81 Ronald Gross, *The Lifelong Learner*. New York: The World Publishing Company 1977, p. 59 cf. Cross, Op. cit.; Atchley, Op cit.

82 Jane Loevenger, *Ego Development*. San Francisco: Jossey-Bass, Inc., 1976, cf. chart on "Conscious Preoccupations," pp. 24-25 cf. Cross Op. cit., pp. 178-179; Kidd, Op. cit., Carl R. Rogers, *On Becoming A Person: A Therapist's View of Psychotherapy*. Boston: Houghton Mifflin Company, 1961, *Carl Rogers on Encounter Groups*. New York: Harper and Row Publishers, Inc., 1970; Fuller, et al., Op. cit.; Atchley, Op. cit., p. 37.

83 Gross, Op. cit., pp. 58-59.

the conflicting demands on their time" and the immediacy of their needs.[84] The prime motivational factor (needs or interests in the present situation) for adults is a priori; whereas, for children the prime motivational factor (needs or interests in the future situation) is a posteriori. The broad categories of adults' needs and interests change with change. In fact, Gross affirms: "adulthood is not a plateau on which the personality formed by earlier experiences is merely played out against changing circumstances. Rather the adult years have their drama of development, their new crises of growth and change which are as decisive as those of childhood and growth."[85]

In Reconciliation theory, we understand the model of self-directed education leans much to the adult model of development, maturation and readiness with motivation to learn. Yet Reconciliation assumes many adolescents of average to above average intelligence may be moved beyond the pedagogical approach to education. From a humanistic and Rogerian standpoint, counseling may facilitate this need in adolescents, especially among the gifted and talented. Often, many adolescents are left out of academic and artistic challenges in the traditional pedagogical model of instruction. Educators and counselor need to be observant and aware of the needs and interests of adolescents so they may be moved into an adult model of self-direction in education and counseling.

As with adults and readily motivated adolescents, Reconciliation induces self-directed learning behavior in the psyche within the context of change. Change reflects crisis and conflict situations, either taking place in settings or overlapping with settings. A crisis denotes the overwhelming impact of change in the subjective context of the psyche; whereas, a conflict denotes, not so overwhelmingly, an impact of change in the context of the psyche. In the life experiences of the psyche, conflicts may be great or small, depending upon the psyche's subjective context. The subjective

---

84 Op. cit.
85Op. cit.

context herein denotes the person's opinion and degree of ability to cope with a particular situation or problem. Malcolm Knowles explains in his formula of motivation that "Needs (Motivating Forces) + Psychological Field = Behavior."[86] That is, in the context of Reconciliation, the educational needs and interests of the psyche being engendered by the crisis situation(s) of the psyche engender learning behavior. Furthermore, Knowles points out that the prime motivating factor (need/interest) is the gap between the "present levels of competency" in light of the future reality of the psyche.

This may also be illustrated with the Hegelian dialectic. Here we are considering the crisis of growing old from Atchley's middle age phase. It is illustrated as follows:

Figure 5: Hegelian dialectic Expressed as Knowing (Learning) Equation

Crisis $\longleftrightarrow$ Present Competency Level $\rightarrow$ Need-Interest $\rightarrow$ Future Competency Level $\rightarrow$ Act of Knowing

Application

Crisis $\longleftrightarrow$ I do not know $\rightarrow$ I need (interest) to know $\longleftrightarrow$ I know $\rightarrow$ I continue to know and shall know.

In this illustration, the motivation force is the gap indicated by Synthesis: Need-Interest. That is, the tension of "discrepancy" between the Crisis and Antithesis: the reality of what the individual is in context (Present Competency Level) results in the Need-Interest to know. In turn, the Need-Interest to know conflicting with the Antithesis, the aspiration or required competency level (Future Competency Level) results in the Synthesis: Act of Knowing.[87]

---

86 Knowles, Op. cit., 1970, p. 81
87 Op. cit., p. 80

Interior Conflict

The learning process of the psyche begins in the conflicts of life, namely, crises situations ranging from the smallest crisis to the greatest. All conflicts present as challenges to the psyche to which, the persona responds or reacts. As noted earlier each antithesis impinges on the psyche the need to learn. Through conflict antitheses emerging from within the psyche or external to the psyche arouses the motivation force that interiorizes the synergism of antitheses through the persona. At the same time, this synergism gives shape to the persona and psyche.

As demonstrated in Figure 5, the persona deliberates in conflict with the discrepancy between the two poles of need/interest: the required level of competency in relation to the present level of competency.[88] The persona, individually or with the help of a facilitator, endeavors to "identify aspirations…and assess [the] present level of competencies in relation to them" so that educational needs will be more accurately defined, thereby, eliciting intensified motivation. Through a series of deliberating conflicts (cf. Figure 5), the persona engages in the act of learning indicative of exploratory and/or problem-solving behavior. With the function of choice, the persona is receiving the perceptual experiences of the psyche. At the same time, the persona is synergizing selected percepts with related aspects of the meaning system. However, negative percepts such as "I don't know," "I don't understand," or "I don't hear you" are placed in a negative system of storage (cf. S-O-R discussion above). Through the life of the psyche though, the persona strives to synergize all aspects of negative storage (meaning) and positive storage (meaning into a meaningful whole (Weltanschauung). In fact, as pointed out in the proposition, Weltanschauung represents the ultimate synergy of one's life experiences or knowledge as depicted in the both-and and either-or paradoxes of psychic Being.

In greater detail, we note that one's Weltanschauung is ultimate-

---

88 Knowles, Op. cit, p. 86

ly attained in the psyche's changing life situations. The crises of the psyche consist of stimuli that elicit within what Brunner calls "intrinsic motives" for learning. [89] These "intrinsic motives" in the individuating psyche among adults and many adolescents are likened to Knowles concept of Need-Interest, the prime-motivating factor. As was said, Need-Interest arises out of or is stimulated by the conflict situation in the setting. The two poles of Need-Interest (the "present level of competency" [PLC]) and the "required level of competency" in the future reality of the psyche [RLC]) icon the past/present and the present/future of the psyche's biography (the biography being the world and life of the psyche).

I have inferred from Knowles the discrepancy between the present and future of the adult represents a driving tension that evokes adult motivation toward what and how he or she will learn. This tension is the prime motivating force behind the act of learning. Through each learning "moment" the conflicts of such antitheses as boredom/curiosity and fear/hope, created by these poles drives and reinforces the learning behavior of the adult psyche. As the psyche gives attention to both the present (PLC) and required levels (RLC) of competency, the tension described compels the psyche to move along the learning continuum. For the psyche, while caught in the midst of this tension through each learning "moment," struggles along the continuum, thereby creating a new present level of competency (PLC) until the ultimate required level of competency (RLC) is met. The learning behavior of the psyche is reinforced upon reaching each new present competency level.

In the adult psyche, these reinforcements enhance the intrinsic motive(s) within the Need-Interest. "Brunner defines an intrinsic motive as 'one that does not depend upon' an extrinsic reward—a reward outside the [learning] activity it impels." The reinforcement of each competency level is, in the subjective context of the psyche, the "newness" of the knowledge gained. This "newness" is the stimulus of the curiosity drive needed to spur the psyche on to the next

---

89 Brunner, Op. cit., pp. 114f.

competency level or learning "moment."[90] The curiosity elicits the reward of discovery which in and of itself is the continuing motivating factor initiated by the Need-Interest.

Weltanschauung

In Jungian psychology this newness is related to each new "group" of the world: "Every new discovery, every new thought," puts " a new face on the world" in the subjective context of the psyche. The objective "world changes its face," and the persona of the psyche grasps this change as an inward "psychic image." For Jung each new group is a new Weltanschauung for the individual. At the same time, as "the picture of the world" changes "at any time" so does "our conception of ourselves change." As each new discovery of the world is made, newness is added to the self-concept. Yet "we must be prepared" for these changes or else we may "suddenly find ourselves in an antiquated world, itself a relic of lower levels of consciousness."[91]

This tension between self and self-concept along with self and world apart from self, created by world and psyche may make or break us (e.g. Roger's discussion of cognitive dissonance).[92] This tension of dissonance is nature's motivating force impelling and compelling the psyche to grow. Jung further believes that the testing of "every new thought" attains wholeness and higher levels of consciousness. They are also maintained by testing "every new thought" "to see whether or not it adds something to our Weltanschauung." Whereas Jung's key to wholeness is depicted in the idea

---

90 Brunner, Op. cit., 1966, pp. 114f. cf. In Brunner, the theory of intrinsic motives in children may reflect the motivation to learn in adults and in this study that same motivation in adolescents

91 Sir Herbert Read, Michael Fordham, and Gerhard Adler (Eds.), *The Structure and Dynamics of the Psyche.* London: Routledge and Keegan Paul, Ltd., 1968, 8, p. 363

92 Kidd, Op. cit., p. 127; Self-concept, http://www.acs.edu.au/info/natural-health/mental/self-concept.aspx (accessed February 01, 2015); Cognitive Dissonance, http://www.learningandteaching.info/learning/dissonance.htm (accessed February 01, 2015).

of testing every new thought, William James' key is that of giving "attention" to every thought.[93]

I concur with Jung that Weltanschauung, as understood in the context of the changing psyche," is a hypothesis and not an article of faith." Jung also understood that a meaning system, in the subjective context of the psyche, is a Weltanschauung and, at the same time, each "new" discovery was a Weltanschauung. Looking at Weltanschauung as a psychoanalyst, Jung equated Weltanschauung with "all conscious awareness of motives and intentions." Closely related to the learning process of the individual though is his statement that "every increase in experience and knowledge is a step in the development of a Weltanschauung."[94]

In the theory of Reconciliation, Weltanschauung denotes the climaxes of each group of composite learning experiences. These composite groups may not be comparatively measured in terms of time or amount, as they will differ according to the subjective context of a learning, maturing, and growing psyche. Each Weltanschauung will depend on how, why, when, and where the psyche learns and the psyche's ability to cope with change; and again, this is according to the subjective context of the psyche and each life situation which is unique to the psyche. Within each psyche, the synergizing of percepts begetting concepts and concepts begetting meaning systems, etc., are icons of each Weltanschauung. Each level of Weltanschauung depicts the psyche's height of understanding or making sense out of experience. Each level depicts the ability to have a heightened understanding of reality. Weltanschauung in the science of learning and education is not a constant mystical euphoria or fantasy. Weltanschauung rather reflects the individual's ability to synergize self and ideal self with one's organism and the world in each of its life situations. In one's Weltanschauung all opposite poles of Being are synergized. This is as if the individual

---

93 James, Op cit., p. 147; Read, Fordham, and Adler (Eds.), Op. cit., 1968, 8, p. 363 cf. Transpersonal Pioneers: William James, http://www.sofia.edu/about/history/transpersonal-pioneers-william-james/ (accessed February 01, 2015).
94 Read, Fordham and Adler (Eds.), Op cit., p. 361.

becomes the synergizing point of the paradox. One's understanding of the world is synergized with the true objective world. Although in constant tension and conflict, the individual's inner self is in balance with the outer self and the world outside of total self.

Overview: Reconciliation and the CAL Model

In summary, the scope of one's learning maturation may be understood overall from a reconciling viewpoint. Patricia Cross depicts a linear model of lifetime change and development regarding the psyche. She refers to this as Characteristic Adults as Learners (CAL): Personal Characteristic Schemata. She posits a steady rise in physical growth with a leveling off from ages 20 through 25. Then a very gradual leveling off occurs until the ages of 55 through 60. At this time, a decline in physical development and vigor becomes apparent. [95]

As for the sociological and cultural life phases in the life of the psyche, Cross depicts these on a totally horizontal level.[96] Her reason for this coincides with my observations that sociocultural change occurs outside of one's self and organism. She writes: "In general, a graph of life phases, while also generally related to age would consist of a series of plateaus separated by transitions. Although one phase leads to another and is incorporated into it, so life phase is higher or better than another, only more appropriate for a given age. Thus the life-phase continuum is essentially horizontal."[97]

---

95 Cross, Op. Cit., p. 237.
96 The horizontal depicts ones learning in the socio-economic and cultural context. This is transitional and is external to the psyche although the psyche's learning and development is impacted by this horizontal factor. In contrast, the vertical depicts the psychological and physical development of the learning psyche. This is also transitional but internal to the psyche. It also impacts on the horizontal and is impacted by the horizontal. Phases of learning as schemata and resultant learning plateaus occur within the range of the vertical and horizontal learning experience.
97 Op. cit.

In contrast to the horizontal level of one's sociocultural phases, personality and developmental traits are depicted as a series of life phases likened to a pattern of ascending "plateaus and transitions." This ascension reflects the ever-increasing dynamics of learning operative in the psyche despite strengths and weaknesses due to physical aging. [98]

Despite the characteristics of aging and the tension of internal and external change, "power" for learning is available to the psyche. From a physical standpoint, weaknesses in seeing and hearing, e.g., may be facilitated for learning through eyeglasses and hearing aids. Learning "in change" may be facilitated by resources whether human or nonhuman via the fields of education and psychology. The dynamics of learning may be facilitated through the constant tension of interaction in the three levels of the learning life cycle. The interrelationships of the Personal Characteristics Schemata is ingeniously depicted by Cross in adjacent horizontal relationships.[99]

In the context of Reconciliation, the dynamics of interconflict among the three schemata are noted. The interconflict is an overview of all conflict and tension in the learning life of the psyche. For example, conflict is understood as a constant within physical, sociocultural, and psychological developmental stages horizontally as depicted in the life transitions of all three schemata. Concomitantly, conflict is a vertical constant among the physical, sociocultural, and psychological developmental stages of these schemata. All of these conflicts compositely elicit forth the various stages or phases of learning development in the psyche. Each learning plateau, in turn, represents a stage in ego-development and in or toward Weltansauung. Weltansauung, in the individual, may occur between a series of two or more plateaus.

The schemata are described in terms of Schema 1, Schema 2 and

---

98 Op. cit.
99 Op. cit.

Schema 3.[100] The first depicts the beginning of the learning function at conception or before birth. When learning before birth, the
child responds to stimuli of the physical and affective of the mother's internal behavior. The second would depict the child's responses
to stimuli in the hospital and home environment. This is inclusive
of the child's growing, attending school and reaching from home
into the world. As the child moves through adolescence and into
early adulthood Schema 3 is realized. Here the impact of sociocultural change and developmental phases is expanding the learning
experiences and development of the psyche. During this period, as
these three schemata expand and converge, Weltanschauung and
ego-awareness are elicited in the psyche.

Furthermore, throughout the learning life of the psyche, once
the organism has evolved into Schemata 2 and 3, these continue
through adolescence and middle adulthood, ages 12-25. From
here they continue in the developmental leveling off period of
the psyche, which begins to decline with ages 55 and following.
Nevertheless, these schemata interact in conflict while synergizing
Weltanschauungs in terms of learning plateaus in the developmental life cycle of the psyche. The tension plateaus of Reconciliation
are depicted as horizontal socio-environmental stimuli generating
conflict on the psyche. Conversely, vertical internal stimuli of the
psychophysical developing psyche interflict with external stimuli.
These reconcile as the Weltanschauung in one's life.[101]

---

100 Op. cit.
101 Relative to what has been said, we postulate the following illustrations.
The following factors depicted are Schema I [S1] (conception, birth and early
childhood), Schema 2 [S2], (later childhood and adolescence), Schema 3 [S3],
(later early to later adolescence, adulthood span), and Weltanschauung [W].

Notes

Part Two

Reconciliation:
Recreating Curriculum and Socio-Culture

And of all illumination which human reason can give, none is comparable to the discovery of what we are, our nature, our obligations, what happiness we are capable of, and what are the means of attaining it.

Adam Weishaupt

Chapter Seven

Recommendations for Reconciliation

A more detailed understanding of learning phases may be gleaned from Loevenger's Stages of Ego Development and Cross' application of them to the individual's aspirations for and outlooks on education and its relation to counseling. Time and space dot permit this discussion here, but the reader may refer to Loevenger's work, Ego Development: Conceptions and Theories (1976) and Cross' work, Adults as Learners (1981).[102] Nevertheless, this study's broad exposition of ego development and Weltanschauung in the light of Cross' schemata, comprising the CAL model, leaves room for the exceptions and "way stations" along the dynamic line of learning development. Says Loevenger: "To telescope the whole sequence of ego development in terms of describing the lowest and highest levels is to miss the spirit" of growth itself. Both psychological and intellectual growth does "not proceed by a straight line from one low level to another higher level. There are many way stations, and they are all important as stages of life and as illuminations of the conception" (of ego development). "In the same sense, [as was depicted in the discussion of Weltanschauung] moreover, there is no highest stage but only an opening to new possibilities."[103] Cross paraphrases Loevenger by referring to Loevenger's stages of development as "milestones of ego develop-

102 Loevenger, Op. cit, pp. 15-26 cf. Cross, Op. cit., pp. 176-177.
103 Op. cit., 1976, p. 26.

71

ment."[104] A detailed study of these stages would certainly facilitate in the development of Reconciliation theory and its application to the individuating psyche.

In conjunction with what has been posited, further recommendations and propositions are posed toward further development of Reconciliation theory. Firstly, Reconciliation is striving toward a harmony of established theories of learning behavior. Of course, such a harmony would require years of study and research by many theorists in both education and counseling fields. Only then may a proper knowledge base be established from which a workable model of learning facilitation is developed.

Secondly, much extensive research will have to be undertaken to adjust and readjust Reconciliation theory to the point that empirical hypotheses may be formulated for future testing and theoretical development.

Thirdly, based upon literature research thus far, the crux from which a theory of facilitation may be developed lies in the area of cognitive dissonance as depicted and treated in terms of conflict, crisis, change and tension of the psyche and its world and their inter-dynamic relationships.

Fourthly, based upon and within the context of the above proposals and postulations, a definite yet dynamic model of developmental learning phases in relation to personality development will have to be ascertained for the sake of developing and adequate theory of learning facilitation for the learning life and development of the individuating psyche.

Fifthly, based upon the principal Proposition treated in Chapter 2 along with the related research and postulations of this study, the theory of Reconciliation plugs into the system of mathetics, a general theory of learning correlating key principles of androgogy

---

104 Cross, Op. cit., p. 176.

and pedagogy. The resultant hypotheses of the Proposition have been tested. Due to time and space, some have been tested more thoroughly than others. Nevertheless, each hypothesis was investigated in the context of established scientific discovery and research and related to the Proposition. As the nature of these five propositions and recommendations indicate, all hypotheses will have to be increasingly investigated for the adjustment, readjustment and development of the Proposition of Reconciliation relative to learning development in education and counseling contexts.

The whole course of human history may depend on a change of heart in one solitary and even humble individual - for it is in the solitary mind and soul of the individual that the battle between good and evil is waged and ultimately won or lost.

M. Scott Peck

Chapter Eight

The Terminus of Reconciliation

Heretofore, we have considered the individual psyche and personality in the theory of Reconciliation. Let us, at this point, consider the aforementioned third proposal and recommendation as the springboard for presenting and understanding Reconciliation in terms of the world of the psyche. As stated: "based upon literature research thus far, the crux from which a theory of facilitation may be developed lies in the area of cognitive dissonance as depicted and treated in terms of conflict, crisis, change and tension of the psyche and its world and their inter-dynamic relationships." A key underlying assumption of this study is that the individual and personality cannot be understood apart from a comprehensive view of the world. We are considering this world in terms of the philosophical construct, the good society. Fundamentally, this study proposes the kind of "good society" that most likely will grow out of transformative education and counseling anchored in Reconciliation theory.

Throughout human history, philosophers and social scientists have concerned themselves with the how in the attainment of the good society. Those ideologies forming the warp and the woof of this treatise depict that in human history the degree of the quality of a society is based on the degree of the quality of individuals comprising its membership. In turn, such quality is indicative of the degree of quality of education provided within the society itself. In essence, this study is based on the assumption that a good society is comprised of good individuals who, in turn, are the products of good education and curriculum. At the same time, we assume that effective counseling facilitates individuals in their learning and educational development. Much time is spent defining and discussing the quality and criteria denoting the good and the methodology for attaining the good—that is, the good referring to the contexts of society, the individual, and education and curriculum; also, the attainment of the good is depicted via criteria for the building a culture—a culture comprising a balance of both unity and diversity as well as generating a cohesive society.

In contrast, this study depicts that such a cohesive society is not to be found in America. Throughout the cause and effects comprising this problem are depicted regarding the contexts of culture and society, education and curriculum and the individual. Of course, every problem elicits needs, and needs in turn elicit responses. Within this study, the shortcomings of traditional empirical science are manifested in multifold dysfunctions due to fragmentation and segmentation in the aforementioned contexts of the said social and cultural phenomena. From the positive standpoint, however, the implied needs generated by these dysfunctions have resulted in the unfolding of a new wholistic behavioral science—a science which takes into account the uniqueness of human nature apart from animal natures and which strives for the synergy of means and ends, as opposed to means from ends, in the method of research and studies involving designated social phenomena.[105] Resultantly, my response has been an attempt to apply the principles of this science to erect a new sense of community within individual

Americans. Furthermore, I have indicated that this purpose cannot be attained with traditional learning theory. Therefore, the attempt is being made to apply the principles of Reconciliation toward a new science of education and curriculum.

---

105 Abraham Maslow cf. Frank G. Goble, *The Third Force: Psychology of Abraham Maslow*. New York: Grossman Publishers, 1970 cf. Abraham H. Maslow, *Religions, Values, and Peak-Experiences*, New York: The Viking Press, 1964

Notes

The only solutions that are ever worth anything are the solutions that people find themselves.

Satyajit Ray

Chapter Nine

Socio-Cultural Dysfunctions and Emerging Solutions

The Ramifications of Traditional Science

Much of contemporary learning theory focuses on the cognitive domain. Basically, the philosophical schools of pragmatism and realism and the psychological school of behaviorism have influenced psychologists and educators. Although much that is positive in the way of teaching methods and approaches, along with an enhanced understanding of human behavior, has been bequeathed to the institution of education; yet these schools have either totally neglected or rejected the affective needs and development of the human psyche. Resultantly, students, over the years, have become socialized into the "Spockian" syndrome of "icy" logic and "cold" empirical methodologies. The same is happening in counseling and therapy as well through the push of insurance companies along with counselors and psychologists toward evidenced based therapies. That is to say, both counseling and learning outcomes must be measured in order to insure reliability and validity. In essence, inductive and empirical sciences have given a psychology that merely regards external human behaviors and an education that is fragmented. Such fragmentation is manifested not only in the division of the human intellect into two distinct domains but also into the segmentation of human knowledge into distinct subject disciplines with no interrelations among them.[106]

---

106 Howard A. Ozman and Samuel M. Craver, *Philosophical Foundations of*

Such segmentation has contributed to much contemporary social dysfunctioning as manifested, for example, in the rise of suicides among our youth of college and high school age and the rise of divorces among adult populations. This has led to the question: are we as a society on the brink of anomie? Agnew reports that subjective anomie will result when success values are too high in comparison to the means values to achieve those goals. Durkheim is cited as stating: "a healthy society sets limits on the goals of its members." Such limits prevent "conditions" from arising that would cause success values to become "limitless".[107] In turn, limitlessness is inferred as a direct manifestation of the societal normlessness existing among American citizenry today. In the Durkheimian sense, increased pluralism in the United States has weakened the social cohesion needed to maintain the balance and order of society. Along with increased pluralism, double digit inflation and increased consumption in conjunction with the rise in unemployment unveils the "the loss of fixed and accustomed points of evaluation," which are characteristic of the "perplexity and instability" in the average American.[108]

In other words, social educators have concluded that the average American is a victim of value confusion. Banks and Clegg cite: "value conflicts are numerous and destructive, and the confusion is so great that many people appear to have no values at all, or endorse ... many conflicting values ..."[109] Consequently, because we have become a value confused society, educators in general, and

Education. Columbus, Ohio: Charles E. Merrill Publishing Company. Second Edition, 1981 cf. Peter H. Martorella (Ed.), Social Studies Strategies: Theory into Practice. New York: Harper and Row Publishers, Inc., 1976; Maslow, Op. cit.; Goble, Op. cit.
107 Robert S. Agnew, "Success and anomie: A Study of the effect of goals on anomie." *The Sociological Quarterly*, 20, 1980, pp. 53-64. cf. Ephraim Mizruchi, *Success and Opportunity*, New York: Free Press, 1964
108 Imogen Seger, *Sociology for the Modern Mind*, New York: Rupert Hart-Davis Educational Publications and the Macmillan Company, 1972, p. 77 cf. Thomas M. Kando, *Leisure and Popular Culture in Transition*, 1980 p. 108
109 James A. Banks, and Ambrose A. Clegg, *Teaching Strategies for the Social Studies: Inquiry, Valuing, and Decision-Making*, Menlo Park, California: Addison-Wesley Company (Second Edition) 1977, p. 408

Third Force psychologists in particular are calling for an unbiased approach to values education. Beck and Maslow both advocate a wholistic and eclectic worldview in education.[110] In essence, this denotes "a broader, more comprehensive, multi-disciplinary approach to human problems" and a means-ends approach to "the identification of ultimate life goals of people in general and the students in particular" rather than the amputated means from ends approach of traditional empirical science.[111] Specifically, "means-centered scientists tend to fit their problems to their techniques rather than the opposite." "Science should be described as the search for [values of] truth, insight, and understanding' and this search cannot be limited to those with highly specialized professional degrees." The trouble with social scientists is that they have "tried too hard to be like physical scientists, with the result that their search for new and better techniques for studying people has been limited." Overall, orthodox science has tended "to put too much emphasis on instruments, techniques, procedures, apparatus, and methods rather than problems, questions, functions, or goals."[112]

Another problem that Maslow depicts is that much of traditional psychology (especially behaviorism) is derived from the study of animals in the laboratory. Shaffer tells us that Maslow, in his early days as "an undergraduate student at the University of Wisconsin," was briefly attracted to behaviorism. He made in-depth studies of primates' behavior in continuity with human behavior, especially focusing upon "the needs for sex and affection." During this process he became "convinced that there existed a fundamental human nature that was unique to homo-sapiens as a distinct species within animal life and that could not, beyond a certain limit, be modified by various social, political, or historical conditions."

110 Clive Beck, "The case for value education in the school." Social Studies Strategies: Theory into Practice. Peter H. Martorella (Ed.), New York: Harper & Row Publishers, Inc, 1976, pp. 116-117 cf. Goble 1970, Op. cit; John B. P. Shaffer, *Humanistic Psychology,* Englewood Cliffs, New Jersey: Prentice-Hall Press, 1978
111 Goble Op. cit, p. 19; Maslow, 1964, Op. cit. cf. Beck 1976, p. 116
112 Goble Op. cit. cf. Maslow, Op. cit.

Lowry pointed out that Maslow's search for "man's higher nature had constituted a remarkably consistent theme in" his (Maslow's) life, for as early as 1928, Maslow had written in an undergraduate paper the following phrase: 'At the moment of the mystic experience we see wonderful possibilities and inscrutable depths in mankind" 113[113]This is quite a contrast to Skinner, who is depicted as describing human nature thusly: "'What is being abolished [through the science of behavior modification] is autonomous man—the inner man, the homunculus, the possessed demon, the man defended by the literature of freedom and dignity.' 'What is left is the real observable human organism who is biological and animal."[114]

With the dawn of Third Force Psychology in exponents such as Maslow, Rogers, Jung, May and other, the emphasis is now to treat the psyche as a whole in its world. The intellect of the psyche is considered in both affective and cognitive senses. The psyche is now "Being-in-the world," i.e., wholly "Being-in-the [total] world." "Being-in-the world" overcomes the subject/object dichotomy that has "plagued Western epistemology since Descartes first attempted to distinguish a mind, or 'soul,' from the body and from the sensory input impinging on it." That is, "the Cartesian conception fragmented what man had initially experienced as a wholistic relationship to the universe into a division between 'inner' and 'outer' reality that isolates the knower from the known and that alienates modern man from the world he inhabits."[115] Rollo May points out that average people's connection with their feelings "is as remote as if over a long-distance telephone. They do not feel directly but only give ideas about their feelings; they are not affected by their affects; their emotions give them no motion."[116] Consequently, May encourages clients to experience the whole self, that is, body and emotions. In achieving consciousness of self, clients "start back at

113 Shaffer 1978, p. 34 cf. Maslow, Op. cit.
114 Ozman and Craver 1981, p. 198
115 Shaffer, Op. cit., p. 22.
116 Rollo May, *Man's Search for Himself*, W. W. Norton and Company, 1953, p. 105

the beginning and rediscover their feelings."

Clients realize "that it is 'I,' the active one, who is doing and feeling: one experiences the affect on all levels of one's self. One feels with a heightened aliveness."[117] Eventually, "the mature person becomes able to differentiate experiences, as is the different passages of music in a symphony."

The Ramifications of the New Science

As with counselors working with clients, educators must start back at the beginning. Teachers and students must realize that they are both thinking and emotive beings. They must learn to feel what they think and think what they feel regarding themselves and their world. They must learn that within them is a "vital force" that can expand their dimension of self and world and that can synergize the antitheses of cosmic Being with the self. [118]

Yet in order for students and teachers "to get in touch" with themselves and their world, social educators must become pioneers in cognitive-affective wholistic education. By cognitive-affective wholistic, I mean that education which includes the whole student and his or her whole world with the latter including both overt and covert curricula. Social educators must become pioneers in this endeavor by first forming a philosophy and/or theory of cognitive-affective learning behavior. And only by forming such a theory can such educators begin to formulate effective methodologies that will truly facilitate wholistic learning in their students. Social educators must feel especially responsible with this task because they, more than other educators, are totally involved in the knowledge and study of people. Peoples themselves are products of their cultures and the latter, in turn, are also products of the former. This also goes with saying that the cement of axiomatic values

---

117 Op. cit.
118 Peter H. Martorella (Ed.), *Social Studies Strategies: Theory into Practice.* New York: Harper and Row Publishers, Inc., 1976, pp. 106-107 cf. May, Op. cit.

holds the building blocks of cultures together, and, in turn, those values come into Being and are sustained by the affective process of valuation within peoples. These cultures also reflect the totality of knowledge and wisdom accumulated by peoples.

Also, today, in progressive schools, social studies have become as such, "an all inclusive curricular area." "This is particularly appropriate since many social studies educators stress that social studies is a practical integration of information drawn from the social sciences and even the humanities rather than merely an umbrella title to encompass discrete disciplines such as history, political science, economics, sociology, anthropology and geography. Indeed, many social studies educators would argue for the inclusion of the academic study of religion as a necessary component of an integrated social studies program."[119] In fact, religion in toto is comprised of the cultural values and valuations of peoples. At the same time, social education.[120] by its very nature draws from all of the humanities and "hard" sciences.

According to Goble, Maslow "lists the following criteria" for all behavioral scientists, and in our case, these criteria apply to social educators and even other educators. First, "The scientist needs to be secure, confident, and mentally healthy in order to have a good perception of the reality he is studying." Second, "the scientist needs to approach problems with an open mind; he needs to be problem-centered rather than ego-centered." Third, "the behavioral scientist needs a broad general knowledge; overspecialization is not productive." Fourth, "the greatest, most successful scientists

generally have had broad interests; some of the outstanding examples are Aristotle, Einstein, Leonardo da Vinci, and Thomas Jefferson." Fifth, "the successful student of human behavior needs to be

---

119 Piediscalzi, Nicholas and William E. Collie (eds.), Teaching about Religion in Public Schools. Niles, Illinois: Argus, Illinois, 1977, p. 5.
120 In this study, social education also includes, psychology and counseling and educators and practitioners regarding both.

more philosophical, more creative, more diverse, more intuitive, to 'see reality whole,' to see all the various disciplines as mutually helpful collaborators rather than separate unrelated specialties." [121]

Maslow also pointed out that the separation of means from ends in traditional science has resulted in the same "dichotomizing trend" in American education. As a result, American education itself has become "conflicted and confused about its far [reaching] goals and purposes." Traditional education has stressed "the acquisition of pure knowledge," namely, "knowledge for its per se value," at the expense of knowledge in the context of its "origins," "motivations," "functions," and "far [reaching] goals and purposes." Too often, students are taking courses because they are listed in the curriculum. They are not given a comprehensive rationale as to the how, why, and where or what "it" was, is and will be in terms of far reaching actions. With this stress on means from ends. Values confusion results in the disciplines taught and studied. As an answer to this problem, Maslow recommends an education that is means-end oriented or, so to say, an education with ends-in-view, as "clarity of end-values makes it easy to avoid" the "mismatchings of means and ends." He continues to say that all knowledge is concerned with arriving at "what have been called 'spiritual values' or 'higher values'" such as justice, truth, beauty, virtue, love, one's relationship to death, the joy and jest of life, and the like. Also, "questions were answered by organized religions in their various ways," but slowly the "answers have come more and more to be based on natural empirical fact and less and less on custom, tradition, 'revelations' sacred texts, interpretations by a priestly class." Consequently, "nineteenth century empirical science is being redefined, reconstructed," and "enlarged" in order to take into its domain the realm of "spiritual values," and "insofar as education basis itself upon natural and scientific knowledge...it, too, will change, moving steadily toward these ultimate values in its jurisdiction." [122]

---

121 Goble, Op. cit., 1970, p. 18.

122

Learn to get in touch with the silence within yourself, and know that everything in life has purpose. There are no mistakes, no coincidences, all events are blessings given to us to learn from.

Elisabeth Kubler-Ross

Chapter Ten

Socio-Culture and Curriculum

A New Purpose for Education

Consequently, social educators must become cultural structuralists. The idea herein is that the walls of our culture are torn down. The building blocks of our culture are lying in piles and are even scattered about on the ground. Social educators must pioneer the reconstruction of our culture. As indicated above, they, more than another other educators, have total cultural awareness. Therefore, they can erect a cultural structure into which future generations may grow. I concur with Counts that although Progressive Education has focused "squarely upon the child" by recognizing "the fundamental importance of the interest of the learner" as well as conceiving of learning "in terms of life situations and growth of character" and championing "the rights of the child as a free personality," such values "constitute too narrow a conception of the meaning of education; [they bring] into the picture but one-half of the landscape."[123] I also concur with Counts that such values are

123 Counts, George S. *Dare the School Build A New Social Order*. New York: The John Day Company, 1932. http://www.scribd.com/doc/20922579/Dare-School-Build-Social-Order-George-S-Counts-1932-31pgs-EDU#scribd (accessed July 2, 2015), pp. 3-4.

"excellent" and I even say further that they are a must, but educators beginning with social educators must complete the other half of the landscape. At this point, education will be given a direction and purpose that is whole and not part.[124]

Here the query may be posed as to how the dignity and freedom of the individual may be maintained and even enhanced if cultural structure is to complete the purpose of education? I have inferred from Counts that no individual is born into the world alienated. The abuse of Progressivism is depicted: "The advocates of freedom often speak of the adult as an alien influence in the life of the child. For an adult to intrude himself or his values into the domain of boys and girls is made to take on the appearance of an invasion by a foreign power." No "child lives in a separate world of his own." "Place the child into a world of his own and you take from him the most powerful incentives to growth and achievement." Evidence from anthropology indicates that the individual "entering the world" "is neither good nor bad; he is merely a bundle of potentialities which may be developed in manifold directions. Guidance is, therefore, not to be found in child nature, but rather in the culture of the group and the purpose of living. There can be no good individual apart from some conception of the character of the good [Italics mine] society; and the good society is not something that is given by nature; it must be fashioned by the hand and brain of man. This process of building a good society is to a very large degree an educational process." And wholistic education takes place only in the real world, viz., among the world of adult values.

But it is this alienation through the abuse of Progressivism that has contributed to the value confusion experienced in American society today. As the mind must have a body and senses to function, so the individual must have a cultural order through which to become. Consequently, the adult world must clarify the degrees of goodness and badness in Being that children may grow into this knowledge. Educators must become cognizant that to to build a culture they must build a culture of children. They need to under-

124 Op. cit.

stand that individuals are the building blocks of cultures and values are the mortar. Great works of art and architecture merely reflect these cultural values. Great works of art and architecture merely reflect these cultural values. They are not the culture itself.[125]

Socio-Cultural Synergy: A New Responsibility for Education

I have suggested that today we do not have a cohesive culture in which to rear our children.[126] Counts suggested that humans by nature need a tradition in which they may fully live and find purpose.[127] This is true freedom. A human without a culture is like a fish out of water. Such a fish is helpless and flips around striving for its life's oxygen, and it will continue to do this as it dies. This is the cultureless anomie of human beings.

Educators in general and social educators in particular must capture this vision in order to sense the urgency to save our fragmented culture. Social educators must lead the way in laying hold on (krateo) society. They must throw off the slave mentality of ancient Rome and Greece and "be prepared to stand on their own feet and win for their ideas the support of the masses of people. In their own lives [they] must bridge the gap [Italics mine] between school and society and play some part in the fashioning of those great common purposes which should bind the two together."[128] But before this can happen, social educators must agree on fundamental ideas and purposes and the values hierarchy underlying them. Without this unanimous consensus, a "conception of the character of the good society" [Italics mine] will not be arrived at and, thusly, social educators will not sense and unite in the high calling of their responsibility—to construct and maintain the social order.

---

125 Goble, Op. cit., 1970, pp. 102-103; Maslow, Op. cit., 1964.

126Ashby, Warren, Violence and Twentieth Century Religious Thought. An unpublished paper presented to the Religious Studies colloquium: Religion 695, University of North Carolina at Greensboro, Greensboro, North Carolina, 1982.

127 Counts, Op. cit., 1932.

128 Op. cit., pp. 27-28.

I have proposed the idea of unanimous consensus among social educators not because I understand they must reconstruct a monolithic culture to implement the needed cohesiveness in American society, but because they must create a balance between the needed unity and existing diversity that is evident in our society today. [129] In addition, the problem with this diversity is not because of the nature of pluralistic diversity itself but the segmentation of the elements of such diversity. Warren Ashby, a professor of ethics at the University of North Carolina at Greensboro, believes that a balanced society is one in which we find "neither too much" order a denoted in traditional cultural monism nor "too little" order as evident in the dysfunctions of today's cultural segmentation. Such cultural dysfunctioning is evident in what Ashby describes as "displaced persons," "dislocated" social institutions, and the segmentation of "objects, purposes, and methods, such as the means from ends dichotomy, all of which are characteristic of today's "age of specialization."[130]   And, of course, this segmentation is evident in Counts' description of the gap between schools and other societal institutions and Third Force Psychologists' descriptions regarding the alienation of the contemporary person from the self and from others and from institutions comprising his or her American society and culture.[131] In essence, Ashby believes that the spatial and temporal distance among and between "objects, purposes, and

129 Cornbleth, Catherine, Geneva Gay and K. G. Dueck, "Pluralism and Unity," *The Social Studies: Eighteenth Yearbook of the National Society for the Study of Education*. Edited by Howard D. Mahlinger and G. L. Davis, Jr., Chicago, Illinois: The National Society for the Study of Education, 9, 170-189.
130 Ashby, Op. cit., 1982, pp. 2-9.
131 Counts, Op. cit. cf. Note: this study advocates the preservation and development of the self that is inherent in small children but later lost in adolescence. As pointed out in the first part of this study, this true self is lost through the contemporary curriculum. As children move into middle school, they are no longer allowed grow into them-selves. Rather they are forced to conform to the curriculum rather than being allowed through guidance to grow into the curriculum. Educators and counselors must enter into their knowledge base and talents while integrating external subjects of the curriculum into their psyches, thereby giving shape and completeness to their personalities. At this point, we must be generating the self-directed student and client.

methods" has become distorted to the degree that life is not able to "'flow' naturally" from "one object/purpose/method to another."[132] This is true according to his understanding, within people institutions, subcultures and nationalities, and among all of these elements, which comprise today's American pluralistic society. Consequently, his answer is that this creative flow must be generated among all elements of our pluralistic culture, fundamentally through a balance of the spatial and temporal distance among "objects, purposes, and methods."[133]

In essence, this balance is attained through a synergetic relationship between unity and diversity. In this way, the unique and rich quality of the American community of cultural diversity will be created and maintained. Cornbleth, Gay, and Dueck pose the concept of multiple acculturation to designate and accommodate "the complexity of human cultures and range of individual differences, and the reality of overlapping group memberships and loyalties."[134] Multiple acculturation denotes the synergism described and is an alternative concept to that of cultural pluralism which traditionally denoted the division and segmentation of American nationalities and subcultures. Furthermore, Cornbleth, Gay, and Dueck write that multiple acculturation "avoids the oversimplification of the melting pot, the exclusionary features of Americanization (Anglo conformity), and the centrifugal forces of cultural pluralism. To the extent that individuals belong to more than one group (ethnic or other), cultural diversity is unlikely to result in divisiveness. As individuals, we are not simply male or female, black or white, Scotch-Irish or Slavic, Christian or Jew, young or middle-aged, liberal or conservative, teacher or student. Multiple group memberships serve as a check on pluralism; the interdependence of pluralities becomes a unifying force [Italics mine].[135]

At this point, we must conclude that social education must agree upon interdependence as the highest value in the

132 Ashby, Op. cit., 1982, pp. 2-9.
133 Op. cit.
134 Cornbleth, Gay, and Dueck, Op. cit., 1981, pp. 182-183.
135 Op. cit., p. 183.

attainment of the good society. Individuals comprising American society, according to Maslow must become integrated psychologically and socially in order that American society may attain cross-cultural harmony or, in other words, multiple acculturation. In the Ashbian sense, Americans need to be educated into the "human need [Italics mine] to relate."[136] That is, only through relations with the self, others, "nature," "human artifacts," and even "death" itself, can human beings find "meaning and depth" in life. In the complexities of relations and interrelations, individuals begin to ascribe to life, purpose, which "include such fundamental aims as feeling, valuing, choosing," knowing, "and acting or being in some way."[137] Conversely, individuals who are not nurtured in love and permitted to develop and become themselves will become "self-centered, avoiding people" finding no purpose of depth in Being.[138] Societal interdependence can only be acquired through implementing the values of relations and interrelations and the facilitation and enhancing of personal choice. Such a society will allow the person to fully become a wholistic individuating self who finds satisfaction in a balanced relationship with self and others regardless of their belief, background, or culture.[139] Maslow believes that "the better society" is the one "which provides an environment encouraging the development of man's potential," and such a society only results from the cultivation of individuating and self-actualizing persons.[140] This society, according to Ashby, helps the individual "to make something fine of life" in that it allows for the "creative order" that results from positive relations and interrelations previously described.[141]

Wholeness and Self-Actualization: A New Curriculum for Education

---

136 Goble, Op. cit., 1970, pp. 27f. and 101f.; Maslow, Op. cit., 1964; Ashby, Op. cit., 1982, p. 3.

137 Op. cit.

138 Goble, Op. cit., 1970, p. 125; Maslow, Op. cit., 1964.

139 Goble, Op. cit.; Hall and Nordby, Op. cit., 1973; Jung, C. G., "The Structure and Dynamics of the Psyche." *The Collected Works of C. G. Jung.* Sir Robert Read, et al. (Eds.), London: Routledge and Kegan Paul, 8, pp. 3-66.

140 Goble, Op. cit., 1970, p. 102; Maslow, Op. cit., 1964.

141 Ashby, Op. cit., 1982, p. 3.

The goal of education, overall, should, therefore, become that which is wholistic, and wholeness results from balance that is characteristic of the synergism between mind and body and thinking and feeling. This synergism is developed in those who have been reared in an environment of strong "emotional support, acceptance, understanding and love." Such children have been cited to have a strong endurance factor in the face of "disease, fatigue, or hardship."[142] "All the evidence suggests that higher status and material well-being do not enhance a child's chances for successful adulthood. Loving relationships form the emotional net into which children and adults can fall."[143] Such relationships result in the "elements" of self-actualization that create "stamina." These are an "open, flexible approach to life; self-esteem; a spontaneous, outgoing temperament; and a minimum of tension, depression, anxiety and anger under stress."[144]

In addition, Maslow "loosely described" the process of self-actualization "as 'the full use and exploitation of talent, capacities, potentialities, etc. Such people seem to be fulfilling themselves and doing the best that they are capable of doing.' The negative criterion was an absence of tendencies toward psychological problems, neurosis or psychosis. The self-actualized person was the best possible specimen of the human species, a representative of what Maslow later came to call the 'growing tip.'" Self-actualized persons are wholistic, but not all wholistic people are self-actualized. Rath-

---

142 Pekkanen, John, "Keys to a longer, healthier life." The Precursors Study conducted by "Dr. Caroline B. Thomas, Professor Emeritus at Johns Hopkins University School of Medicine. *Readers Digest*, March 1983, pp. 25-32. The study was begun "in 1946 and today is the longest ongoing one of its kind, is to find early clues to disease, particularly the heart." The sample comprised of 1, 337 Johns Hopkins medical students. "Besides certain standard physical tests information was gathered on genetics, demographics, family history and metabolic factors. A battery of psychological tests probed attitudes and personal characteristics. The questionnaires covered childhood, family life, goals and emotional outlook. Habits such as cigarette smoking and coffee and alcohol consumption were also recorded. Since graduation, the students, now medical doctors, have sent back questionnaires annually."
143 Pekkanen, John, Op. cit., 1983, p. 30.
144 Goble, Op. cit., 1970, pp. 23-25; Maslow, Op. cit., 1964.

er self-actualization is the result of becoming. Wholistic people are moving toward the fullness of maturity ("the development or discovery of the true self and the development of existing or latent potential"); they are becoming "fully human." In essence, self-actualization is the goal, and individuation, becoming and maturing designated the dynamic process toward the goal. In the realm of wholeness, Being denotes self-actualization and becoming denotes the maturational process. According to Maslow, self-actualizers "are usually sixty years of age or more" and "most people do not belong in this category" but much of this latter group may be designated as becoming.[145]

Maslow's theory of self-actualization was the result of his studying the most psychologically healthy individuals who have ever lived as opposed to Freud, who based his whole psychological theories on the study of neurotics and psychotics. According to Goble, "the study of these individuals, their habits, their characteristics, their personalities, their abilities led Maslow to his definition of mental health and his theory of human motivation." His studies opened "a whole new area to behavioral science." He made case studies of such people as "Abraham Lincoln, Thomas Jefferson, Albert Einstein, Eleanor Roosevelt, Jane Addams, William James, Spinoza, Albert Schweitzer, and Aldous Huxley."[146]

Education that is wholistic will expose students to leading men and women who are characterized as wholistic and self-actualized in the varied academics and fine arts. Also, students will "be taught that the most important values are found in human relationships."[147] Consequently, students will be encouraged to learn the values of wholistic diverse people demonstrated in biographies, autobiographies and highly integrated group relationships. Respecting integrated group relationships, students comprising such groups will interact with one another and the facilitator of learning[148] by means of the Socratic dialectic of question-answer.

145 Goble, Op. cit., 1970, pp. 23-25; Maslow, Op. cit., 1964.
146 Op. cit., p. 24.
147 Pekkanen, Op. cit., 1983, p. 30.
148 Knowles, Op. cit., 1980; Brubaker, Op. cit., 1982.

These students will represent diverse social and cultural backgrounds. The Socratic dialectic will be applied also in the context of the disciplines themselves. From what has been depicted in this study, cognitive-affective wholistic education will result in the student who is exposed multiculturally, multisocially and multidisciplinarily. In such a learning context, the student's choice mechanism will be enhanced and facilitated. As choice is developing, the individuating psyche will be manifesting the synergism of thinking and feeling, i.e., the synergism of the cognitive and affective domains. Furthermore, the confrontation of the student with problems and issues in such diversity will result in the psyche's motivation to continual inquiry and discovery. In turn, cognitive-affective maturity will result in valuations demonstrative of increased eclectic understanding of diverse bodies of knowledge and increase human compassion and understanding.

In the aforementioned learning situation, proper learning facilitation will result in the students developing a sense of self-worth, tolerance, respect and love for the freedom and individuality of others. Students, through value-cognition, will individuate toward "self-fulfilling" and self-directing persons.[149] The learning facilitator coordinates the experiences that his or her students encounter. In the Jungian sense, the facilitator is aware that as food is "consumed by the physical body and is converted into biological or life energy, so experiences are 'consumed' by the psyche and converted into psychic energy." The facilitator is aware that as "drugs ... produce changes in psychological functioning so thoughts and feelings appear to affect physiological functions." In this context, Jung defines a value as "a measure of the amount of energy that is committed to a particular psychic element." In other words, "when a high value is placed upon an idea or feeling it means that this idea or feeling exerts considerable force in influencing and direction one's behavior." Essentially, the facilitator of learning is exposing and directing the student's cognitive-valuations toward "psychic elements" in the curriculum. Also, the curriculum, in this case, is

---

149 Knowles, Op. cit., 1980.

totally meeting the needs and Meta-needs of students by providing a social, physical and cultural environment that sets "preconditions for need satisfaction, freedom, justice, orderliness" and "challenge (stimulation)." In this way, wholistic growth will be facilitated for the first several generations after which an integrated and wholistic American culture will be come manifest for the generations to follow. The gap of school and society finally will close.[150]

Be that as it may, a curriculum that provides a wholistic learning and maturational environment will permit the facilitator of learning to direct students toward Being-values of self-actualization. In multidisciplinary learning situations that are socially and culturally integrated, differences will gradually synergize from antithesis to synthesis—from hate and prejudice to love, compassion, understanding and acceptance. The American tradition of basing success on the amassing of capital and the acquisition of goods and assets will give way to revaluing safety, security, and physiological needs as means toward acquiring the social and family values of love, belongingness and self-esteem. The upholding of self-actualized people (previously mentioned) as examples will provide what Jung would term the psychic elements that transform physical energy into psychic energy. These psychic elements are synonymous with the needs and meta-needs of the Maslowian hierarchy that occur in the life and learning environments of students discussed here. The curriculum, and ultimately the society, will facilitate the acquisition of Being-values by allowing the psyche to increase the amount of psychic energy directed toward the social and meta-needs of the hierarchy. In the meantime though, presenting the characteristics of self-actualization (Being-values and meta-needs) in biographies and autobiographies, in human interrelations, and in academic and fine arts, will enable students to become cognizant of their value. In fact, Being-values, such as truth, beauty, justice and love have been the goals throughout human history of

---

150 Jung, 8, Op. cit., 1960, pp. 3-66; Hall and Nordby, Op. cit., 1973, pp. 59-60 cf. Goble, Op. cit., 1970; Counts, Op. cit., 1932, Ashby, Op. cit., 1982; Knowles, Op. cit., 1980.

knowledge in general and science in particular.[151]

Finally, as students are reared in the diversity of a wholistic curriculum, they will begin to synergize the antitheses of life. As synergizing takes place students become integrated human beings. Integration results from and in "peak experiences." Jung employs the concept, Weltanschauung. That is, students develop a heightened sense of consciousness and reality as they enter into union with themselves and the world around them. Such peak experiences result in a experience of newness that comes from fulfilling meta-needs.[152] Also, as students grow from Weltanschauung to Weltanschauung, they enter into contemplative states in which universal axioms become immediate realities. Maslow describes such perceptions as being "less distorted by desires, anxieties, fears, hopes, false optimism, or pessimism." He "termed this non-judgmental type of perception [as] 'Being-cognition or B-cognition.'" "It is a passive and receptive type of observation" also called '"desireless awareness.'" But Maslow points out that "Being-cognition alone is not enough" because "it can lead to too great a tolerance, too much indiscriminate acceptance, and loss of taste." Consequently, he concludes that the fully mature individuals must "perceive in two ways" contemplatively (Being-cognition) and decisively. When cognition shifts to the second kind of perception, decision, judgement, condemnation, planning, and action become possible." Here we have the essence of the development of cognitive-valuation processes within the psyche. That is, education that is wholistic develops the faculty of choice in relation to the processes of Being-cognition and decisiveness. And the exercise and development of these processes throughout the years of school leads the psyche from peak experience to peak experience on to self-actualization and wholeness.[153]

---

151 Jung, Op. cit., 8, 1960; Hall and Nordby, Op. cit., 1973; Goble, Op cit., 1970; Maslow, Op. cit., 1964

152 Berger, Op. cit., 1963, p. 61.

153 Goble, Op. cit., 1970; Maslow, Op. cit., 1964; Jung, Op. cit., 8, 1960.

There can be no knowledge without emotion. We may be aware of a truth, yet until we have felt its force, it is not ours. To the cognition of the brain must be added the experience of the soul.

Arnold Bennett

Chapter Eleven

Conclusion

In conclusion, the necessity has arisen to point out the fundamental assumption upon which this study is based as an attempt to apply practically the Proposition of the theory of Reconciliation to the learning and developmental process. Also, the research and theory comprising this study are by means complete but are strongly suggestive of the effectuality and potentiality of Third Force Psychology as applied to the structuring of a wholistic psyche and socio-culture through the vehicle of a new education and curriculum. Of course, this new education and curriculum is summed up in the theory of Reconciliation, which by its very nomenclature suggests a philosophy and methodology for synergism of the antitheses of Being. In general, this philosophy and methodology is being applied to the segmentation and antitheses of objects, purposes, methods, concepts and ideas within the psyche that, in turn comprise the institutions of our contemporary American socio-culture.

Methodologies proposed begin with the goals of cognitive and affective synergism within the psyche, then the synergism of the psyche with his or her world, and ultimately the synergism of socio-cultural groups, which undoubtedly comprise the institutions of society. Methodologies proposed are based upon the assumption that the higher or spiritual values (Meta-values) provide the cement of cultural building blocks, which, in turn, elicit the cohesiveness of societies. The locus of such values is found in the hearts of human beings in dynamic interactions comprising globally diverse cultures and societies. This is the rationale for applying Jungian, Maslowian and other humanistic theories of human valuation and motivation as the means through which students and clientele may attain Reconciliation of self and culture.

Although the writer is aware that much positive research has been done proving that the higher values discussed herein are to be found in positively strong human relationships, he remains compelled to explore further ramifications of the research presented in this study for the purpose of adjusting and readjusting his theoretical assumptions and propositions. Concomitantly, the writer is in need of exploring many of the Maslowian case studies regarding self-actualized human beings and even carrying on many case studies of his own. Nevertheless, much of the research accomplished thus far may provide positive assumptions along with a theoretical framework that provides educators in general and social educators in particular with guidelines for creating a wholistic curriculum that will ultimately elicit a wholistic psyche and socio-culture.

In this study, the terminus of reconciliation is to be realized through the synergism of antitheses within the psyche and world (socio-culture) through education and counseling approaches that lead clients and students through enhanced self-awareness. In turn, through self-awareness and self-reflection client's and students are able to develop a clarity regarding self and other in the midst of struggles and conflict. At that point, they enter into effectively positive relations with self and other. In this situation, they see needs and strengths of self, relative to other. Thus through awareness of their own knowledge base, relative to strengths and needs, they become empowered key into additional knowledge through the curriculum and therein are able to shape and reshape their psyches. Concomitantly, they become artists of self and personality and ultimately artists and architects of a wholistic culture and society.

All in all, they are shaping autobiographies and personalities as works of art and Being. Such education and counseling fosters self-direction and creativity in the psyche of student and client. Educators and counselors that are truly mentors and facilitators model the self-direction and creativity for students and clients while engendering the creative work of shaping students and clients as works of art. They engage with student and client autobiographies and ultimately guide students and clients through mentoring and facilitating toward creative works of self-actualization.

The ultimate end of learning, creativity and development is the realization of Meta-needs and thereby Meta-values. Although Maslow presents this process as a hierarchy of the psyche and society moving from basic needs to meta-needs, the writer sees this process as circular. Because human beings are multifaceted being made up of the many dimensions of matter and spirit, they are meeting multifaceted needs in these two basic domains. This writer does not limit the human psyche to a mere bipartite or tripartite nature of mind and body or mind, soul (spirit) and body. To set limits on the psyche's structure is to truly limit the potentiality and actuality of the human being.

Thus in educating and counseling the psyche, needs are encountered where they are at Therefore, educating and counseling involves developing needs in process from where they are at. From a circular standpoint, one may have physiological needs, but at the same time, such a person will have needs of love and belongingness. Of course, if that person senses the need for belongingness, he or she most likely wants to feel and be safe. At the same time, such a person may struggle with suffering and deprivation of basic material needs. He or she may be persecuted or imprisoned, yet that person most likely could totally despair or seek for higher meaning, the raison d'etre. In essence, needs and values make the psyche into a person, as he or she is shaped by beliefs about self, other and world. To empower such a person as a creative being means that educators and counselors empower that person with creative self-direction in shaping self and world.

~~Fini~~

Bibliography

Agnew, Robert S. "Success and anomie: A Study of the effect of goals on anomie." The Sociological Quarterly, 20, 1980

Arndt, William F. and F. Wilbur Gingrich, A Greek-English Lexicon of the New Testament and Other Early Christian Literature. Chicago: The University of Chicago Press, 1957.

Atchley, Robert C. The Social Forces in Later Life: An Introduction to Social Gerontology. Belmont, California: Wadsworth Publishing Company, 1972.

Banks, James A. and Ambrose A. Clegg, Teaching Strategies for the Social Studies: Inquiry, Valuing, and Decision-Making, Menio Park, California: Addison-Wesley Company (Second Edition), 1977.

Beck, Clive, "The case for value education in the school." Social Studies Strategies: Theory into Practice. Peter H. Martorella (Ed.), New York: Harper & Row Publishers, Inc, 1976.

Berger, Peter L, Invitation to Sociology: A Humanistic Perspective. New York: Doubleday and Company, Inc., 1963.

Biehler, Robert F., Psychology Applied to Teaching. Boston: Houghton Mifflin Company, 1974

Bornstein, Mare H. and William Kessen (Eds.)., Psychological Development from Infancy: Image to Intention. New York: John Wiley and Sons, 1979.

Brubaker, Dale L., Curriculum Planning: The Dynamics of Theory and Practice. Dallas Texas: Scott, Foresman and Company, 1982.

Brunner, Jerome S., Toward A Theory of Instruction. Cambridge, Massachusetts: The Belknap Press of Harvard University Press, 1966.

Carterette, Edward C. and Morton P. Friedman (Eds.), Handbook of Perception: Historical and Philosophical Roots of Perception. New York: Academic Press, I, 1974.

Chaplin, James P. and T. S. Krawiec, Systems and Theories of Psychology, Third Edition. New York: Holt, Rinehart and Winston, Inc., 1974.

Cognitive Dissonance, http://www.learningandteaching.info/learning/dissonance.htm (accessed February 01, 2015).

Cornbleth, Catherine, Geneva Gay and K. G. Dueck, "Pluralism and Unity," The Social Studies: Eighteenth Yearbook of the National Society for the Study of Education. Edited by Howard D. Mahlinger and G. L. Davis, Jr., Chicago, Illinois: The National Society for the Study of Education, 9, 170-189.

Counts, George S. Dare the School Build A New Social Order. New York: The John Day Company, 1932. http://www.scribd.com/doc/20922579/Dare-School-Build-Social-Order-George-S-Counts-1932-31pgs-EDU#scribd (accessed July 2, 2015).
Cropley, A. J., Lifelong Education: A Psychological Analysis. New York: Pergamon Press, 1977.

Cross, K. Patricia, Adults As Learners. San Francisco: Jossey-Bass Publishers, 1981.

Discovery Learning (Bruner), http://www.learning-theories.com/discovery-learning-bruner.html (accessed January 02, 2015).

Douglas, Mary, "The abominations of Leviticus," http://kodu.

ut.ee/~cect/teoreetilised%20seminarid_2011/teoreetiline%20 seminar%2015.03.2011/Douglas.pdf (accessed December 24, 2014).

Educare, http://en.wiktionary.org/wiki/educare (accessed December 23, 2014).

Facilitating learning and change..., http://infed.org/mobi/facilitating-learning-and-change-in-groups-and-group-sessions/ (accessed December 22, 2014).

Fuller, George, James Calhoun, and Martin Schulman, Understanding Psychology, Second Edition. New York: Random House, Inc. 1977

Ginsberg, Mary Lou, Kenneth Henry, and Dennis Krebs, Understanding Psychology, Second Edition. New York: Random House, Inc., 1977

Girard, Rene, Violence and the Sacred. Baltimore: The Johns Hopkins University Press1972.

Goble, Frank G., The Third Force: Psychology of Abraham Maslow. New York: Grossman Publishers, 1970.

Grant, Michael, The World of Rome. New York: World Publishing Company, 1960

Gross, Ronald, The Lifelong Learner. New York: Simon and Schuster, 1977.

Hall Calvin S. and Vernon J. Nordby, A Primer of Jungian Psychology. New York: The New American Library, 1973

Henry, Virgil, The Place of Religion in Public Schools: A Handbook to Guide Communities. New York: Harper and Brothers Publishers, 1950.

Hewitt, Paul G., Conceptual Physics: A New Introduction to Your Environment. Fourth Edition. Boston, Massachusetts: Little Brown and Company, 1981.

History of Bar Mitzvah, http://www.myjewishlearning.com/life/
Life_Events/BarBat_Mitzvah/History/Bar_Mitzvah.shtml (accessed December 27, 2014).

Hurlock, Elizabeth B., Developmental Psychology. New York:
McGraw-Hill Book Company, 1968.

Instructional_Design: Facilitation Theory, http://teorije-ucenja.
zesoi.fer.hr/doku.php?id=instructional_design:facilitation_theory
(accessed December 22, 2014).

Israel, Abrahams, et al., Jewish Values. Jerusalem, Israel: Keter
Publishing House Jerusalem, Ltd., 1974.

James, William, Psychology. New York: Association Press, 1963.

Jerome Bruner, Constructivism and Discovery Learning, http://
www.lifecircles-inc.com/Learningtheories/constructivism/bruner.
html (accessed January 02, 2015).

Jung, C. G., "The Structure and Dynamics of the Psyche." The
Collected Works of C. G. Jung. Sir Robert Read, et al. (Eds.), London: Routledge and Kegan Paul, 8, pp. 3-66.

Kando, Thomas M., Leisure and Popular Culture in Transition,
1980

Knowles, Malcolm S., The Modern Practice of Adult Education:
Androgogy Versus Pedagogy. New York; Association Press.

Knowles. Malcolm S., The Adult Learner: A Neglected Species.
Second Edition. Huston, Texas: Gulf Publishing Company.

LeBon, Tim, Viktor Frankl and Logotherapy, http://www.timle-
bon.com/frankl.htm (accessed December 22, 2014).

Loevenger, Jane, Ego Development. San Francisco: Jossey-Bass,
Inc., 1976.

Maslow, Abraham H., Religions, Values, and Peak-Experiences.
New York: The Viking Press, 1964.

May, Rollo, Love and Will. New York: W. W. Norton and Company, Inc., 1969.

May, Rollo, Man's Search for Himself, New York: W. W. Norton and Company, Inc., 1953

Martorella, Peter H., (Ed.), Social Studies Strategies: Theory into Practice. New York: Harper and Row Publishers, Inc., 1976.

Mizruchi, Ephraim, Success and Opportunity. New York: Free Press, 1964.

Neither, http://www.thefreedictionary.com/neither (accessed December 14, 2014)

Ozman, Howard A. and Samuel M. Craver, Philosophical Foundations of Education. Columbus, Ohio: Charles E. Merrill Publishing Company. Second Edition, 1981.

Pekkannen, John, "Keys to a longer, healthier life." The Precursors Study conducted by "Dr. Caroline B. Thomas, Professor Emeritus at Johns Hopkins University School of Medicine. Readers Digest, March, 1983, pp. 25-32. The study was begun "in 1946 and today is the longest ongoing one of its kind, is to find early clues to disease, particularly the heart." The sample comprised of 1, 337 Johns Hopkins medical students. "Besides certain standard physical tests information was gathered on genetics, demographics, family history and metabolic factors. A battery of psychological tests probed attitudes and personal characteristics. The questionnaires covered childhood, family life, goals and emotional outlook. Habits such as cigarette smoking and coffee and alcohol consumption were also recorded. Since graduation, the students, now medical doctors, have sent back questionnaires annually."

Person-Centered Therapy, http://en.wikipedia.org/wiki/Person-centered_therapy (accessed December 22, 2014).

Piediscalzi, Nicholas and William E. Collie (eds.), Teaching about Religion in Public Schools. Niles, Illinois: Argus, Illinois, 1977.

Purity and Danger, http://www.bc.edu/bc_org/avp/cas/his/
schloesser/HS041-042/fall/w04/resources/DOUGLAS_Puri-
ty-Danger.pdf , p. 54 (accessed December 24, 2014)
Read, Sir Herbert, Michael Fordham, and Gerhard Adler, Eds.,
The Structure and Dynamics of the Psyche. London: Routledge
and Keegan Paul, Ltd., 1968, 8.

Rogers, Carl R., On Becoming A Person: A Therapist's View of
Psychotherapy. Boston: Houghton Mifflin Company, 1961.

Rogers, Carl R., Carl Rogers on Encounter Groups. New York:
Harper and Row Publishers, Inc., 1970.
Seger, Imogen, Sociology for the Modern Mind, New York:
Rupert Hart-Davis Educational Publications and the Macmillan
Company, 1972

Self-concept, http://www.acs.edu.au/info/natural-health/mental/
self-concept.aspx (accessed February 01, 2015).

Self-Directed Learning, http://www.selfdirectedlearning.
com/teaching-self-directed-learning-tools/articles/a-new-theory.
html (accessed December 22, 2014).

Shaffer, John B. P., Humanistic Psychology, Englewood Cliffs,
New Jersey: Prentice-Hall Press, 1978.

Slaate, Howard A., The Pertinence of the Paradox. New York:
Humanities Press, 1968.

Stage Theory of Cognitive Development, http://www.learn-
ing-theories.com/piagets-stage-theory-of-cognitive-development.
html (accessed January 03, 2014)

Synergy, http://en.wikipedia.org/wiki/Synergy (accessed December 24, 2014).

What is Gestalt Therapy? http://www.gestalt.lv/eng/therapy
/what_is_gestalt_theory/ (accessed December 22, 2014).

The process of individuation, http://www.soul-guidance.com/

houseofthesun/individuationprocess.htm (accessed December 28, 2014).

The Structure and Dynamics of the Psyche: The Collected Works of C. G. Jung. Sir Robert Read, et al. (eds.). London: Routledge and Kegan Paul, 1960, 8:3-36.

Transpersonal Pioneers: William James, http://www.sofia.edu/about/history/transpersonal-pioneers-william-james/ (accessed February 01, 2015).

Index

A

B

C

F

Facilitate 12, 27, 38, 44, 58 , 70, 81, 94
Facilitator 44, 60, 92, 93, 94
Free will 43
function 12, 34, 41-44, 51, 60, 66, 86

G

Gerontologists 55
Gestalt 15, 29, 106
Goble 31, 74, 77,79, 82, 83 , 87, 90, 91, 92, 94 , 95, 103
Good society 73, 74, 86, 87, 90
Good society 73, 74, 86, 87, 90
Good Society 73 , 74, 86, 87, 90
Grant 37, 103
Gross 11, 57, 58, 103

H

Hall 43, 79, 90, 94, 95, 103 , 106
Harmonization 3
Havinghurst 50, 51
Healthy society 78
Hegelian dialectic 13, 16, 24, 53, 59
Henry 22, 35, 36 , 103
Humanistic 16, 24, 79, 101, 106
Hurlock 33, 104, 113

I

identity vi, 3, 6, 7 , 28, 50, 57
Identity Crises 57
Inclusive 4, 5, 31, 66, 82
Individuation 37, 41- 43, 47, 49, 53, 92, 106
Inductive and empirical sciences 77
Innocent 6
Interdependence 89, 90
"Intrinsic motives" 6i

J

James and May 45

K

L

M

N

O

About the Author

As a counseling professional, the author has experienced the value and power of autobiography writing. He has continued to grow and mature in it as a musician, writer and counselor. Through his education and struggles in everyday life, he has continued to grow in the traits of is life that have shaped his personality as a counselor, mentor, artist. The road to professional counseling grew out of his education experience as a teacher, musician, minister, and priest. The author works with the student age population growing out of his educational background and licensure as a teacher of grades K-12, but specializing with grades 9-12 and later those of college age. His emphasis of study began in junior high school with

the study of music and later becoming a piano major in college.

Colophon
Tites in Gabriola
Text in Minion Pro
Book set in Adobe Indesign CC

Gabriola is a display typeface designed by John Hudson. Named after Gabriola Island, in British Columbia, Canada, it is primarily intended for use at larger sizes, but can also work well in short passages of text. The Gabriola font can add elegance and grace to titles, subheads and other situations in which a more decorative style of type is appropriate.

The design of Gabriola was inspired by an idea from music: that the same melody can be played in multiple modes, each with its own expressive characteristics. Gabriola was developed with advanced OpenType features and has been optimized for advanced ClearType rendering to improve legibility on screen.

t.

www.ingramcontent.com/pod-product-compliance
Lightning Source LLC
Chambersburg PA
CBHW020535290526
45786CB00002B/892